Horseman,
pass by!

Horseman, pass by!

Irish pages

MICHEL DÉON

translated by Clíona Ní Ríordáin

THE LILLIPUT PRESS
DUBLIN

First published 2017 by
THE LILLIPUT PRESS
62–63 Sitric Road, Arbour Hill
Dublin 7, Ireland
www.lilliputpress.ie

Copyright © Michel Déon, 2017

ISBN 978 1 84351 708 5

1 3 5 7 9 10 8 6 4 2

ACKNOWLEDGMENTS
Published with the generous support of
The Ireland Funds, the French Embassy
in Ireland and the Alliance française, Dublin.

Set in 12.5pt on 17.5pt Fournier by Marsha Swan
Printed in Navarre, Spain, by GraphyCems

for Alice Déon

Foreword

ONE MORNING in the late 1990s, the postman brought a cream-coloured envelope with the name Michel Déon scrawled above the return address of the Académie française. I immediately recognized the author of *The Purple Taxi*, the 1970s French film and fiction classic that had been my first introduction to the eest of Ireland, when I was a student at the Sorbonne.

I was delighted to receive the hand-written card, praising my reports from Paris in *The Irish Times*. I telephoned Déon at his home in Tynagh, County Galway, and we agreed to meet the next time he visited Paris. A lunch at the Brasserie Lipp was, as the Hollywood movie says, the beginning of a beautiful friendship.

Michel's wife Chantal was a 'horsey woman,' he told me, like Anne, the mysterious young woman in *The Purple Taxi*. In *Horseman, pass by!* he pays tribute to Chantal, identified as 'C', 'sitting regally on her saddle with that grace that has never left her'.

Through Chantal's fox-hunting with the Galway Blazers, the first people the Déons met in Ireland were members of the dying Anglo-Irish aristocracy. 'Ireland had slowly destroyed them,' Déon writes, 'taking their virtues from them and distilling in them the slow poison of its laziness in a curious seesaw movement.'

When I visited Michel and Chantal at the Old Rectory we went for long walks in Portumna Forest accompanied by E.T., their pet Weimaraner. Like the narrator and his young American friend in *The Purple Taxi*, we often walked in silence. We lunched at Moran's on the Weir, where Déon had also feasted on oysters and Muscadet with the late John McGahern.

Déon has a great talent for friendship. I loved to hear of the times he spent with Jean Cocteau, Coco Chanel, Salvador Dali, Françoise Sagan … In his company, one touched all of France's twentieth-century artistic and literary history.

Déon's two most successful novels, *The Wild Ponies* and *The Purple Taxi*, were partially or wholly set in Ireland. He then neglected Irish themes for close to two decades. Published in France in 2005, *Horseman, pass by!* is his distillation of decades of memories in Ireland.

Many of the Irish people Déon meets in this book are, like him, solitary creatures who seem compelled to walk the roads and pathways of the West. 'To be honest, I like walking by myself to talk to myself in my head,' he tells Australian tourists, descendants of one of Lady Gregory's servants, on a visit to Coole Park. He is eager to escape their company, because he wants to contemplate Yeats alone.

Déon was sitting on the front lawn at Tynagh one summer afternoon while bees buzzed in the fuchsia bushes. A frail man of about forty, with tight black corkscrew ringlets for hair and a striped blue suit, approached him. 'I am a poet. I'm going to write poems and since you are a very well-known writer I would like you to help me to get them published,' says the interloper, who spends his days writing poems in his head as he walks. When they meet again fifteen years later, the 'poet' has not yet committed poems to paper.

Déon asks an alcoholic, homeless man whom he drops off in Ballinasloe what he does while he's walking. 'I think. I think about the choices in life. You think better when you walk,' the man replies.

Ciaron, a sedentarized traveller, angers his wife by walking to Galway, returning days later with a calf and a horse. Leslie R., a dog-lover and sometime walking companion, takes Déon on a quest for the grey fox said to harbour the banshee soul of an old woman who was refused a Christian burial.

Déon elevates Big Sarah, a homeless woman who lost her husband and six children, to the status of myth. 'For centuries, she had been walking the roads of Donegal, Mayo and Connemara, miming an imaginary conversation with the dead,' Déon writes. Big Sarah rested in 'grocers-cum-haberdashers-cum-post-offices among the crazy bric-a-brac that disappeared each year to make way for faceless shops'.

In those days, Déon notes, people were kind-hearted. *Horseman, Pass By!* is a lament for the Ireland he knew and loved. Tim, the postman from Ballindereen, is replaced by a man on a motorbike, who doesn't waste time talking about the weather. Villagers shun baskets of apples, offered in an orchard because they prefer their apples sealed in cellophane from the supermarket.

On a Yeatsian pilgrimage to Sligo, Déon asks: 'What had become of the hedgerows of hawthorn, brambles and fuchsia?' Garden gnomes dot the lawns of bungalows that spring up like poisonous mushrooms.

'Oh my dears, what are you doing to one of the most poetic countries in Europe?' is Déon's *cri de coeur*. 'Prosperity has come crashing down on Ireland like paedophilia on base clergymen. Would Yeats recognize his beloved Sligo?'

Before a turf fire in Achill, Déon meets a red-haired young Irishman in an Aran jumper who rails against the cliché that all Irish people have red hair and freckles. The writer looks around the room and counts three other redheads. Stereotypes, he warns us, tend to be true.

But it would be a mistake to dismiss *Horseman, pass by!* as a Frenchman's clichés about Ireland. Déon's vignettes have the stark beauty of Paul Henry's paintings of the West. That the Ireland he describes is threatened, renders his vision all the more poignant. His carefully observed pen portraits of Ulick O'Connor ('a mixture of a dandy and a tramp') and John McGahern belong in the annals of Irish literary history.

Though Déon recounts at least a half-dozen deaths in *Horseman, pass by!* they are, as he writes, 'not tragedies, just pages which are turned, and soon turn to dust'.

Now in his ninety-eighth year, Déon wanted an English

language translation of his Irish memoir. His one hundreth birthday will mark a half-century since he, Chantal and their children made their first tentative move from the Greek island of Spetsai to Ireland. Alice Déon was a boarder at Our Lady's Bower in Athlone, and Alexandre a day student at Portumna Community School.

Greece obsessed him, Déon notes; Ireland kept him. The translator Cliona Ní Ríordáin and The Lilliput Press have fulfilled his wish to leave a book thanking Ireland, and that is cause for celebration.

Lara Marlowe
Howth, County Dublin
September 2016

Preface

MORE THAN fifty years ago, while living on the Greek island of Spetsai in the Aegean Sea, where all is grace and beauty, my young wife and I listened to friends vaunting the attractions of an Irish winter, with their stories of fox-hunting (for my wife) and snipe and pheasant hunting (for me).

In France at that time the Nouveau Roman reigned triumphant. Not alone was it ruining French literature but it blocked any possible way forward, since it fenced literature in within a rule-bound space, the antithesis of the romantic freedoms demanded by a novelist's imagination. As I had not yielded to the fashion, I was frequently labelled 'reactionary' at best (and at worst) because of my earlier novels and travel writing.

In this impossible impasse I could have lost the freedom that mattered to me above all others. And so it was abroad, away from the sordid infighting of kitchen sink literary politics (to which, happily, I am utterly indifferent) that I thrived.

We arrived in Ireland on a whim, though we had already been charmed by the place during earlier successful weekend visits spent in the great outdoors. We immediately understood that our new life would be spent in a precious haven where we would find peace, and independence of spirit, all the while remaining French, and from France.

Of course, my lines on Ireland do not aspire to equal those written by great travel writers. They do, however, record the grateful thanks of a French writer who has learned to love Ireland and appreciates its open-mindedness, independence of spirit, its courage, its hopes and its humanity. I have written these pages with complete honesty, while keeping uppermost in my mind the fact that France has forever been steadfast friend of the green isle of Erin.

Michel Déon
Old Rectory, Tynagh, Co. Galway
September 2016

Horseman,
pass by!

Cast a cold eye
On life, on death,
Horseman, pass by!
    —W.B. Yeats

2.

I HAVE BEEN OBSESSED with Greece – it will always be in my thoughts, bringing back memories and penetrating my books with its light – but it's Ireland that has kept a hold on me ... Well, for the moment in any case. Who knows what tomorrow will bring. Ireland is here in front of me as I write these words, outside the window, the red horizon, still heavy with bluish clouds, pushed by the wind towards the vast Atlantic. In a second, just as the Pacific swallows up the *Nautilus* with its lights blazing at the end of *The Mysterious Island*, our house will disappear in the depths of a starry night, a sign of the cold weather and the frosty fields that await us when we wake. I count the years: fifty since my first visit, and we spent more than thirty autumns and winters here before dropping anchor in this watery land. Almost a third of my life. Why? How?

In my earliest memories of childhood I can still hear my mother speaking of her Irish blood – of an ancestor of ours, Joachim Crofton de Motte O'Connor. Five generations lie between that mythical ancestor and my mother's tales. No doubt the drop of Irish blood has been diluted, but it exists and has been carefully nourished by my mother, who took me to the theatre to see plays by Wilde, Shaw, O'Casey and Synge. I can't say whether this modest start to my education really affected me but I adored Swift and, later, Wilde and Shaw, whose sarcastic views are the only possible response to the suicidal nonsense in the world. I have written elsewhere about the impact of Joyce's *Ulysses* on me, the inspiration for so many of my dreams.

What can you make of this drop of Irish blood in the veins of a Frenchman, who had no real reason to go and live in the Republic of Ireland after spending so many years in his beloved Mediterranean cradle? I can't explain it. I can simply bear witness to an attraction, to which I, like others, have succumbed. In any case, I pursued this interest to its logical conclusion by coming to live on this island.

Although Lawrence Durrell also claimed Irish ancestry through his mother, he never yielded to the same temptation, though it does seem that there was a kind of extrapolation on the part of the author of *The Alexandria Quartet*. We, his readers, friends and defenders against the enemy (Peter Levi) lying in English critical ambush, believed him all the more naively because we could feel a volubility in his multi-faceted art – novels, stories, poems and plays – inherited from Irish verbal delirium, which oscillates between joy and despair. He had found it intuitively, and applied it to other horizons – Egypt, Greece, Arabia, Provence – the passionate lyricism of the Gaels, emended, it is true, by a healthy dose of humour, and the rare gift of seeing people not as they are but in the role they play for their great puppeteer, the novelist.

Actually, his Irish genes were no more conclusive than mine, and it took the patient research of an American academic, Ian Mac Niven, to reveal that Durrell could boast only one Irish great-grandmother. One-eighth thoroughbred. Not bad, still, you might say. It was in Avignon, in the Palace of the Popes, on the floor of Miracles, with about thirty participants from lots of different countries, sitting around the same horseshoe-shaped table. There was a pretty girl in black shorts and a tee-shirt, with long blonde hair that covered half of her face when she leaned over her notes, but luck was not on my side because I was sitting far away from her. On my left sat a twenty-stone, hard-bitten Durrell fan straight out of a Fellini film, swathed in a vast sari of her own design. She had slipped me her calling card stating that she was professor of poetry at the University of San Diego; later, she thrust a slim volume of poems that she'd inscribed to me in my pocket.

'It's five dollars,' she said. 'If you translate it into French, ask my agent for the terms and conditions.'

And she gave me his card too. But Mac Niven continued persistently in his demonstration and as it went on, it seemed more and more that Durrell's quarter of Irish blood was being drained to an eighth, and by the end of the conference there was hardly any left at all. There is a lesson to be learnt there about the vulnerability of writers and the humiliations that await them beyond the grave when people have rummaged in their drawers and hung out their dirty linen. Don't we novelists, the tight-walkers of the imagination, have the right to invent a private life of our own after loaning so many lives to others for which we receive no gratitude? Don't we of all people have the right, during or after an existence devoted to make-believe, to use a little of that make-believe for our own benefit? How many hours, days, weeks, how many enquiries at the Indian or English Office of Public Records did it take Ian Mac Niven to retrace a complicated genealogy and to deduce ... Well what did he deduce? I would have approved if he had concluded that the world of the novelist ends up taking him over, that between his fiction and his own life, where the frontiers of writing cease to exist. If Durrell had convinced himself that he had Irish blood, his work had drawn from this adopted imagination a frenetic need for liberty. But Mac Niven was having none of that. Biographers are pitiless detectives and their passion for the truth, be it sordid or minor, is equalled only by their myopia.

Why and how does the Irish nation have a fascination with the literary and political history of the Western World, when in actual fact its major works, like its politics, are recent? The Celtic Revival dates from the end of the nineteenth century, and its political freedom from 1921. Where is the truth in the clichés that smother the country and to which, in moments of weakness, it sometimes conforms? In a little B&B on Achill Island, where we holed up soaking and happy after a day's walk under one of those exhilirating downpours that feel like a purifying shower or an immersion in the Ganges, five or six guests were pretending to warm themselves around a turf fire, with a smell of smoke and undyed wool drying near the hearth. A young man in an Aran sweater pushed some seats in the direction of the frozen strangers: 'I could hear your French accents.'

'Probably because we are French.'

'I teach French in a school in Athlone. This year Camus' *L'étranger* is on the syllabus.'

Because of the way he said 'Camouss' and 'L'étanglais', I initially underestimated him, but the depth of his knowledge of that slice of French literature was moving in that lost guesthouse on a storm-whipped island. The three women knitted or finished their embroidery; the men smoked their pipes, their legs outstretched towards the flickering blue and yellow turf fire.

'I really love France and I hope to go there one day,' our new friend said, with a warmth such as French people, who understand that they are not looked up to as much as they once were, can only hear with a tug on the heartstrings. 'Yes, I love the French language, but why do your writers insist on saying that all Irish people are freckled redheads? You've travelled all over Ireland and you can see for yourself that even if it is true from time to time, it's hardly without exception.'

The remark was partly true. At that stage I had written nothing about Ireland yet — I caught up some years later —

I could plead my innocence, but the question disarmed me. The young teacher, who spoke my language with as much passion as ignorance of its pronunciation, was himself a furiously coppery redhead, and in the little room with its battered seats and its awful lace curtains, yellowed by the smoke of the turf where we were trying in vain to warm ourselves up, there were three other redheads, not gingers but real carrot-tops. They were an overwhelming majority. The situation was becoming complicated: this very friendly young man didn't know the colour of his own hair, and didn't see that there were three other redheads in the room; without understanding a word of our conversation, they nodded in sympathy with the idea. The longer I looked at him, the redder I found his hair, and with the three beatifically smiling redheads in their battered armchairs, I decided (without owning up to it) that all Irish people are redheaded. How was I to say this to my new friend, whom, by the way, I never saw again, without humiliating him? As a true polemicist, he would have replied that, since we cannot see ourselves, we have no reason to believe a third party's judgment on our physiognomy, or our intelligence, or our talent.

2.

DURING THE FIRST MONTHS of our first trial period in Ireland
(1969), we rented Kilcolgan Castle, which lies deep in Galway
Bay on the edge of a ria populated by swans, seagulls, redshanks,
flocks of crested lapwings, with curlews endlessly repeating
their names, and yellow-beaked puffins limping along in search
of mussels. I may seem knowledgable about them today, but
it was far from true at the time and I was frequently frustrated
by my ignorance. The diversity of the bird world demanded
a precise vocabulary. From Paris, I was sent the *Guide des
oiseaux européens*, an incomparable source of information for a
bird-lover. Not only are the illustrations perfect but they give
the names of the birds in several languages: English, German,
Dutch, Swedish, Italian and Spanish. Of all these nomenclatures,

the French language probably represents the most picturesque: *circaète jean-le-blanc* sounds softer on the ear than its English *short-toed eagle*, and *lagopède des saules* is a sweeter term than the German *Moorschneehuhn*.

No one can write at a constant pace all day, and my bird-breaks are pleasant memories of those months of work. I had chosen a narrow boudoir (to put it nicely) for my office, which was easy to heat with a gas-fired radiator. Its only window looked onto the ria, filling and emptying with the tide. We had been warned that at floodtide the ground floor of Kilcolgan Castle would disappear under three feet of water for several hours. The floor, the meagre sticks of furniture and the wallpaper all bore the traces. The terrible state of the sofa, whose springs stuck out from the worn stuffing, the fake ebony desk, the shaky chair, and the hunting scenes on the walls, cut out from English magazines, are best forgotten. With her characteristic energy, C. had removed layers of dirt and salt from the windowpanes so that, from my vantage-point, I could survey the multiple mood changes of the watery green landscape and the grey or even coal-black sky – the occasional patch of lovely blue was too fragile to last more than a few minutes. Despite its flattering name, even now it's been restored, Kilcolgan Castle is not very lordly in appearance. I suspect it was the nineteenth-century folly of some Irishman who wanted to give himself airs and graces, with its solid two-storey keep flanked by two sorry-looking wings. The owner, the Honourable Mrs A., rented it to us for six months while she remained invisible in a kind of glacial garage. That summer, as he was passing through Spetsai, Desmond, Knight of Glin, in response to a question about the ladies of Galway said: 'Mrs A.? Hmm, there are lots of witches in the neighbourhood.'

The arrival in the courtyard of our overloaded car, with two children impatient to see their new home, disturbed a cloud of crows that had been perched on the chimneys and trees. Mrs A. did not appear on a broomstick. She did not look the slightest bit like a witch. I would have said a suffragette myself – short grey hair in a boyish cut, a long hooked nose, and cheeks that were rosy from the morning's two-ohour march with her dog. Was she a widow? Probably, but you can't ask questions like that. In any case, she enjoyed a robust friendship with an Englishman, George S., who lived in a very comfortable mobile home that was easy to move around the meadows he rented at the edge of the bay. George S. was dying of cancer, slowly, with periods of remission that allowed him to rustle up excellent dinners to which he invited us on several occasions. He was a cultured man, rather depressed, no doubt, but consoled by the wines that he had sent down from Dublin. I have never heard anyone say the words 'Château Beychevelle' with such greedy happiness, as if he was about to enter into communion with it. During my morning walks, if I passed by his mobile home and the weather was good enough for him to sit out on the steps facing the bay, we would exchange names of authors and memories of French books that he had read in translation, but since the first day I avoided the banal 'How are you?' to which he had replied, 'Still alive.' His last wish was to own a Laguiole knife. When I brought one back from a brief trip to Paris in exchange for a penny, I saw I had made him happy. He died shortly afterwards, and I hope that in his coffin a kindly soul placed his knife and a bottle of Beychevelle.

That year, to my indifference, we experienced the worst winter we have ever seen in Ireland. It rained ceaselessly, tornadoes felled the beautiful trees that surrounded us, and a flu, said to have come from Hong Kong, confined all four of us to bed in one room, where our neighbour, the delightful Dr Lydon, who looked like Fred Astaire, tended to us with a bag full of mysterious medicines. The drugs were incapable of relieving our horrific headaches and the children's vomiting, but his compassion and his calm certainty that we would emerge from this hell finally cured us of the episode; when I said indifference, my only explanation can be my race to finish *Les Poneys sauvages*. For years, I set aside, took up again, took apart and rewrote the novel into which, as I entered my fifties, I wanted to put my all – the story of my generation, Europe struggling with civil war and setting fire to the world, ideological choices, friendship and the neutral ground on which, terrified by the idea of Armageddon, men of goodwill recognize and make peace with each other. Through one of those premonitions that so many other books have given me, five years previously I had imagined that my characters would be wrapped up in the finished article in Ireland, a land I scarcely knew, and so it was that, guided by obscure forces that have played such a role in my existence, I found myself attracted to the exact décor I had imagined in *Les Poneys*. It was so thrilling that it negated the offensive weather and the discomfort of the ugly 'castle', which was all so unlike our perfect winters in Greece, where we were thinking of returning as soon as I had finished my novel. Was I indulging in a bout of asceticism? That would be an overstatement, but self-castigation is a good thing. It also gave me the impetus I needed for the end of the book, as I was depending on the shock of the encounter with this new, rougher world, and on whichever unknown telluric force it was that had made this Atlantic island a hotbed for writers, poets, artists and wild dreamers.

The children went to school in Clarenbridge, where the nuns looked after them with a firm hand; they would sometimes lock Alexandre into a cupboard, much to Alice's shame, so as to continue with their teaching in peace. The few months they spent at school there were a great success; they caught the measles, mumps and chickenpox in quick succession – the best education at that age. Thanks to our neighbouring friends, C. was able to ride again and I was full of self-reproach for having selfishly deprived her of her passion during all those years spent on our rocky Greek island.

And so it was that one morning the Galway Blazers invited her to hunt with them; they were to meet at Paddy Burke's famous pub near Kilcolgan.

The Blazers were famous for having joyfully set fire to the pub on their return from a great day's hunting, but when? It couldn't have been yesterday, and during the years of English occupation the Irish had taken a liking to setting fire to things. In Clarenbridge, we were assured that the owner of the pub that bore his name would not allow himself to be roasted as easily as all that. Known throughout the west of Ireland for his volatile temper and his fiery outbursts, he would chuck out the men he didn't like the look of, refuse to serve women at the bar, and had stuck a 'No Children Allowed' sign up over the door to the premises. I write this many years after his death, and his pub has since become a restaurant that is neither very good nor very bad, but where people dine in a semi-darkness that has the merit of dissimulating whatever is swimming in one's plate. The Galway Bay oysters that they serve aren't bad, but not as good as those to be had in Moran's at the Weir, less than a mile from Clarenbridge. The mystery of the oyster beds! At the time, nobody went to Paddy Burke for his oysters; people went there for the masochistic attractions of a bar owner who, while being out of sorts and angry, can display fraternal and complicit sentiments to serious clients. When you were admitted to the inner circle, you felt you really counted.

Without a word of complaint from the motorists, about thirty horses blocked the traffic on the main road between Galway and Limerick. Still locked up in their van, the pack of hunting dogs barked heartrendingly. The drivers had parked the vans and were enjoying a pint with the riders. The riders were already mounted – redcoats, black jackets, a priest in a riding jacket and top hat, farmers in jeans and wellington boots riding hacks, or piebalds or semi-retired thoroughbreds. The spectacle was reminiscent of a nineteenth-century caricature (the pursuit of the inedible by the unspeakable, as Oscar Wilde would have it) but the scene took place in Ireland where a liberty of dress code and speech reigned, a gaiety that removed all pretension from a ceremonial so stiffly respected in Britain and France. I took great pleasure in seeing C. sitting regally on her saddle with that grace that has never left her. A waiter carrying a tray of ports, pints of beer and stout and whiskies, zigzagged between the riders. Still on the ground in a red coat and dress boots, a man with a youthful face that belayed his fifty years was taking bottles and glasses out of the boot of his car and offering them round – glasses for the members of the hunt, cups for those following on foot. All those different spirits and beers provoked an immediate reaction – the men gave their horses to the grooms and went to relieve themselves in the river in the shade of a little bridge while the women queued up at the entrance to the pub's outdated 'facilities'. The pack was set loose and when the master sounded the horn, the riders trotted across a side road leading to a coppice. With perfect calm or calculated indifference, the man in the dress boots closed the boot of his car and jammed on a riding hat, which was held in place by a tight strap that cut through his double chin. Beside him, a woman in a yellow oilskin who was clearly older than him held the impatient horse by its bridle. Nimbler than one would have believed, the man swung himself into his saddle and passed me.

'Hello, you must come to see us. Anthony L. has told me about you. We'll expect you tonight at Woodlawn. I'm Derek T.'

He trotted off to catch up with the hunt. His accent was so strong when speaking French that one might have thought it affected. The woman, who a moment earlier had been holding the horse as her husband stood a round to the assembled riders, joined me.

'Anthony told us that you hunted at his place in Cumbria. He's an old friend of Derek's. This is a map to get to Woodlawn. Seven o'clock. It won't be black tie, just a gathering between friends. I'm Pat T.'

While the invitation lacked affectation, it sounded like an order, given in a superior tone that in English society, to which she obviously belonged, is a reminder of hierarchies to ignorant outsiders. In my head, I politely calculated that she was ten years older than Derek. Shortly afterwards, we learned that she had had several husbands – well, at least two – before marrying Derek, the last gentleman of leisure in our part of the west of Ireland.

Woodlawn turned out to be a huge eighteenth-century manor house, which was impossible to heat and needed a battalion of servants to look after the wood fires in each room and in the corridors. The walls were not entirely bare and, partly to mask the yellowing dusty spaces left by the seizure or sale of family portraits, the Ts had hung some engravings representing rustic landscapes filled with cows and sheep – presents from passing guests that had been left in the attics for ages. At nightfall we could barely make out the park, or what remained of it, but the following month, when we were invited over for lunch, we were treated to an apocalyptic sight: only the roots of the most precious trees, which an ancestor had brought back from the East and the West Indies, remained; the land around the park had been sold a while ago to the small farmers whose vice was tightening around Woodlawn. As for the house itself, in full daylight it wept distress in its one-eyed splendour, with most of its windows boarded up, but on our first night-time visit it retained all its arrogance, surrounded as it was by a landscape of bogland and poor fields. The dining-room was reminiscent of a stage set, with false doors leading on to wings encumbered with machinery, fake furniture, walkways and pulleys. However, unlike the stage set, the entrance hall and the corridors were dramatically empty. In the drawing-room, which was still complete with its worn furniture, there remained a full-length portrait, dating from the 1920s, of a beautiful woman in jodhpurs and a riding jacket, with her hand on the shoulder of a chubby-cheeked little boy who had long hair like a girl. Despite the puffy face and squinting eyes, you could still tell Derek was the little boy in the painting, but was it really him in the purple velvet smoking jacket with silvery grey silk lapels, dinner suit trousers and black slippers embroidered with foxes' heads? Mark Bence-Jones had just published *Twilight of the Ascendancy*, to which Derek had added a tragi-comic chapter of his own.

I cannot remember the other guests – probably members of the Galway Blazers, who kept up a conversation about the day's hunting that was far beyond my understanding. Pat got up to serve and Derek busied himself uncorking bottles and filling glasses, sometimes just his own glass, especially because he drank faster than us. His face turned puce; he lit cigarette after cigarette without touching anything on his plate, his speech was halted by a chic stammer, which he seemed to forget from time to time. When the cheese arrived at the end of the meal with a carafe of port, he served himself a big glass, passed it along to his left and enquired after his dogs. Pat reassured him: 'They're fine.'

And as I was holding the carafe out to her, she took it, served herself and pushed it towards the person on her left, although I had hoped to fill my glass. In responce to my awkward gesture she said, 'You missed your turn. Wait for the next round.'

Shortly afterwards, indisposed by the vodka, white and red wines, port and mediocre cognac, I asked for the lavatory.

'It's far away, on the first floor and badly lit. Take a candle. The best thing to do is to go outside. But not on the porch please. Walk as far as the grass.'

Outside you could see nothing either. I was lucky not to miss a step and I stopped a couple of paces farther along. I was about to relieve myself when a thunder of barking broke out. If I had gone on two metres, I would have sprayed the wire netting of the beagles' kennels.

'You woke the dogs,' Pat said reproachfully on my return, in the tone of a young mother whose incontinent guest has woken her quintuplets.

Derek was having a conversation that he alone seemed to be following. By the light of the candelabras we could see his Chinese shadow dancing on the naked wall: his neck hunched into his shoulders, his outstretched hand carrying a reddish stain – his glass of port. A detail that had escaped me was the superb tear that showed up on his elbow. The smoking jacket was visibly new and unless he had been attacked by a dog, this tear was the master's own work. Did Derek still have a valet to wear his shoes in for six months before he wore them himself? Surely not. So I could imagine him dipping his shoes, made by a famous bootmaker, in water, leaving them to steep and then polishing them himself as a gentleman should.

Each time I think about Derek T. – and I do so more often than I would have expected on that particular night – each time I come to the same sad diagnosis: the end of his race. He was the perfect symbol of the middle English aristocracy, who had arrived in Ireland centuries earlier as conquerors following in Cromwell's footsteps. Ireland had slowly destroyed them, taking their virtues and distilling in them the slow poison of its laziness in a curious seesaw movement. Some of the Anglo-Irish ascendancy had reacted by moving into the opposing camp, bestowing their loyalty with brio on the other country at great cost to their own lives, serving the perpetual rebels who dreamed of independence with their political talent, intelligence and cynicism, which had been seriously lacking before, smothered by a thousand bloody revolts. Derek was not an imbecile, but perhaps he had decided to behave like one, taking refuge in futility and living with the flag flying high even though the ship had sunk several decades ago. Ireland was emerging from a long tunnel and was going to join the European Community. The death warrant of the gentlemen of leisure had been signed. Derek could not ignore it. We discovered soon afterwards that he was selling everything. That dinner was the last for his silverware, which was leaving for a Dublin auction house the following day. The rest – very little – was to follow, but he carried on hunting, running up bills at the tailor and the wine merchant and planning a trip to Greece all the same. When disaster knocks on the door, hope and peace are to be found only in a game of smoke and mirrors.

At one point during this first dinner Derek disappeared, and as it was getting late I suggested to C. that we return home. We had an hour's drive ahead of us on an icy night. Pat asked us to excuse Derek: 'It has been a long day for him. He might have gone to bed.'

As we swung the car round in front of the porch, the headlights lit up the kennel and the beagles' eyes shone fiercely in the dark. Lying down with the dogs, the nape of his neck leaning against the kennel, was Derek, sleeping with his hands joined on his stomach.

As long as you didn't see him too often and viewed him as a distraction from your usual pursuits, Derek was quite interesting. To a writer, I mean. Evelyn Waugh could have slipped him into one of his novels just as he was, and the readers would have smiled at the caricature, only slightly more exaggerated than the characters in *Vile Bodies*. A buffoon, yes, but also a pathetic illustration of a class of society who, seeing their social status and privileges collapse, continues to behave as if nothing were wrong, without changing course. If Derek was convinced by it deep down, this self-imposed discipline – futility on principle – not only made it impossible to question or feel sorry for him, but also made a spectacle of him. When would he crack?

When Woodlawn was sold at auction for a few thousand pounds, which would scarcely calm the worries of the tailor, the mechanic, the wine merchant and the horse-hire, the Ts rented a flat in the outhouse of a neighbouring castle in Gort. Less grand, but appearances were kept up. The big portrait of Derek and his mother couldn't have been hung on the wall of a flat with such low ceilings, and I bet that it is now in the United States where, among the new classes, they have need of ancestors.

We would have declined an invitation to dinner had the Ts not promised us William King, a former submarine officer who had just finished a solo round-the-world tour on a kind of junk-rigged schooner armed with an automatic pilot of his own invention. This handsome sailor, with his bronzed skin, white curly hair and a nose unworthy of such a masculine face, proved to be a disappointment, as is the case for most solitary sailors (with the exception of Olivier de Kersauson), but perhaps he was subdued by the presence of his bluestocking of a wife, Anita Leslie. Compared with the adventurous face of her husband, she was – with her toad's eyelids, sloping chin and horse's teeth – as ugly as she was snobbish. The first question I wanted to ask was, 'Why, Bill King, after your first trip around the world, instead of coming back to Plymouth, where you started, didn't you carry on going like Moitessier did?' Anyone else would have swung around on their axis without touching the soil, rather than falling back into the clutches of that female dragon, who immediately put us in our places with spontaneous disdain. Wasn't she related to Churchill? All I had to do was read *The Marlborough Set*, the third and last volume of which she had just published. My confession that because I worked a lot, and read mostly in French, the saga had escaped my notice earned me a reply whose significance I still meditate on today: 'Of course, it's not surprising you are a *professional* writer.'

Perhaps she meant that, besides the army and politics – but only at the highest level, there is inconsiderable agitation on the part of the 'professional' plebs, of which I was one, for if rumour was to be believed I lived off my books, and earned a good living at that. How vulgar!

I tried in vain during the dinner to make King speak, but either shyness or reserve on the eve of the publication of his memoirs (*Adventures in Depth*), the details of which he did not wish to reveal, made him let his wife speak for him. So we didn't hear his version of the story of his shipwreck – how he had remained there with the keel in the air for a good quarter of an hour, hands on deck, feet against the roof, certain that if one wave had turned the *Galway Blazer II* over like a pancake, the next one would set it to rights again. Or of another incident that happened off Auckland: a rare attack by a sperm whale had punctured the hull and forced him to keep a starboard tack for more than a hundred miles so that the boom would allow him to stuff the hole with everything he found underfoot before returning to Auckland. The man who had gone through all that, and more, was there in front of us, self-effaced, buoyed up only when talking about his sheep farm at Oranmore at the far end of Galway Bay, in the meagre domain that he had inherited from his grandfather.

It was a damp squib of an evening but the idea of bringing us together came from a good intention, and I was thanking the Ts for it when they announced their plan to spend some time in Crete in September. Well, yes, we would be in Spetsai at that time, and of course they would be welcome to call on their return journey.

THE SALE of Woodlawn left them with a little money, and their life of pleasure was to continue with rough patches and brief returns to fortune. The last of these returns – we heard about it quickly in the closed society of the Galway Blazers – was due to the sale of Derek's Purdeys, two fine shotguns that dated from the beginning of the twentieth century, made by the greatest hunting gunsmith in the world, the last toys a gentleman would agree to part with.

THEIR ARRIVAL in Spetsai was a perfect set piece. He was wearing summer clothes, which were looking a bit shabby, redolent of better days under imaginary tropics; she was decked out in vaporous veils. I think they were happy, finding friends of friends among the cosmopolitan set of Spetsai and on the neighbouring coast. Derek wanted to play backgammon and I warned the Greeks that in his innocence and taste for panache he certainly didn't have the means to lose. A little conspiracy meant that catastrophe was avoided. My modestly stocked wine cellar was quickly emptied; the passing boats had to be called on. In the daytime the temperatures of 35° to 40° meant that our friend was threatened with apoplexy. In the evening when dined on the Argolidan coast, he would pick up for two or three hours, and then, as he stepped out of my Boston Whaler, we would put him into the hands of a coach-driver and ask him to drop Derek off at the top of the steep hill outside the house, where once inside he would collapse into an armchair on the patio and beg for a last nightcap. The stars, the movement of the boats in the old port, the perfume of the garden – jasmine and mirabilis – the enchantment of the Greek evenings, I wonder if he was sensitive to any of it. He was one of those beings who lived in a bubble and could travel the earth without ever tasting the strange or the marvellous.

On his departure he showed me a pound sterling note.

'Is this enough for the maid?'

'She would prefer a ten pound note, no doubt.'

'Good God, I thought domestics were paid very little in Greece.'

'That has not been the case since the departure of the Turks.'

He always had that firm and comfortable certainty that money corrupted the 'lower classes'. But could you blame him? Brought up in that way, he was a kind of old fossil who never questions what he has been taught: a gentleman doesn't dirty his hands by working. That is where honour takes refuge when there are no wars left.

A few weeks later, we met in Athenry at the first hunt of the season for the Galway Blazers, which was the start of the joys of autumn. In a sports-coat (with a torn pocket this time), corduroy trousers and a tweed cap, Derek was standing behind the boot of his car offering drinks to the members of the hunt and, generously, to all those who passed by. As usual, he held forth with wide gestures and a braying voice: 'I'm waiting for a new horse. I'll be with you next week.'

People complimented him on his complexion – the traces of the Greek sun were still visible.

'We plan to go back. A little hot though, Greece ...'

He shook hands with me, which he didn't often do: 'You must come to dinner next week.'

That very afternoon a gamekeeper found him in the forest in Gort, a shotgun still hugged to his chest, his head blown to pieces by the explosion of a number 6 cartridge, unrecognizable, a dog resting at his feet. 'The honourable solution', as the English say. He left nothing, not even his head, which was a mash of flesh, bone, brains and hair. Absolutely nothing. An absolute void, as if he had never really existed, which is perhaps true, except that we shall always remember the comedy of the morning, his gaiety, the promises he made on taking his leave, the glasses of whiskey offered to all who came, the horse that was awaiting the next meet with the Blazers. If the decision to put an end to the sordid accumulation of debts dated from several weeks back, it was really a great performance. Torn between a world caught in its traditions and a world in full development, Derek had jumped into the void.

The question I still ask myself is whether Pat knew how bad their situation was, whether she had the slightest suspicion of the ending that Derek had foreseen for himself. She probably had no idea. It's possible for two beings to live side by side, love one another without needing to talk about it, out of propriety and incapacity to show their feelings, then discover through a dramatic turn of events that the other has a secret life. Those with *savoir-vivre* wouldn't recommend it.

In the humble oratory of the Church of Ireland a pastor read a passage from the Bible and gave a brief sermon, to which none of the participants paid attention. The coffin lay on two trestles between the aisles, devoid of flowers, with just his hunting hat and a Christless cross. His body had been put into the box without the head, but it was the head we searched for in our still fresh and already fading memories – did he ever have a head? Nonetheless, when the chips were down he showed courage and inflicted on himself a terrible death, burying with him an age that would never come back, an age full of vanity, but which, through its vanity, left you reeling in the void. I have always been interested in the last survivors of a mode of life condemned by the march of the centuries, and have collected tomb-closing books since I was a child: *The Last of the Mohicans* by Fenimore Cooper, *Les aventures du dernier Abencérage* by Chateaubriand, and the magnificent *Qui se souvient des hommes* which Jean Raspail devoted to the last Alacalufes of Tierra del Fuego. They are not tragedies, just pages that are turned, and soon turn to dust.

Out of necessity and with a less strict regard for the code that Derek had respected to the letter, Pat found work and became a cook, or, if we dress it up, her talents were called upon during cocktail parties. She prepared *petit-fours* and *mignardises* without losing face. Wearing an apron and rubber gloves, her hair caught in a madras, she would come out of the kitchen to shake hands with the guests who were her friends and to drink a glass of white wine before returning to the stove.

3.

IN KINVARA, the fortified castle of Dun Guaire has resisted the cruel march of time and the neglect of men. Proudly planted at the water's edge on a creek in Galway Bay, watched over by supercilious swans, Dun Guaire defends the port and its cheerful houses, which are brightly painted in hues of chocolate brown, oxblood red, daffodil yellow, sky blue and even cloudy white. The fortress no longer wards off invaders or rebels; today it is preserved – what a waste! – to distract tourists in the evenings with a traditional banquet held on the top floor, roughly hewn wooden benches, huge tables on which the serving girls (I'd like to call them *comely maidens*, an impossible cliché but what other phrase is there to use? and they are comely, as is often the case in Ireland) in medieval costumes place bowls of steaming soup or some kind of broth, which they ladle into tin dishes. Dressed in long gowns of plum or apple velvet, decorated with lace at the wrists and the neckline, two harpists accompany themselves as they sing old ballads. The Lord of the West blows every day in the bay and the young girls are all rosy-cheeked. As soon as the audience is present, the lights are switched off and the candles are lit. My knowledge is based on hearsay and the castle's advertisements. There are takers in high season, but it doesn't last very long.

It is not this flashy cut-out castle that I am thinking about, but Lady H, who had renovated Dun Guaire and lived there. This enigmatic creature must have been heading for her eightieth birthday when I first saw her at an early morning meet of the Galway Blazers; she was the only one to ride side-saddle, and was so elegant that she seemed to have emerged from a full-page illustration of *Horse and Hound*: her hair was an aristocratic grey, of course, and she was discreetly made up, but just enough for one to glimpse under the ravages of time the traces of the austere beauty she once was. Disdaining the protective helmet, she wore a chic tricorne hat like those that figure in nineteenth-century engravings. A black frock-coat was cut close to her narrow waist and enclosed an arched centaur-like upper body. The wide riding habit hid her legs, of which we could glimpse only her ankles, laced up in carefully polished boots. For the dare-devils in the crew, she inspired consideration without the slightest trace of mockery. On foot or by car, I sometimes came across the hunt and I could see that when faced with a difficult or dangerous obstacle (hedgerows, gates, fences, walls or streams) the others waited for her or went ahead to show the way to her horse. When she jumped a dry stonewall – if she stayed in her saddle – her body became disjointed and you could swear that if she had been blown backwards her head would have come unscrewed and rolled onto the grass or on a carpet of dead leaves in a copse. If that had happened, nobody would have doubted that the rider would have kept on with the hunt. A gallant member of the team would have found the time – even when the tally-ho was being shouted out – to pick up the unscrewed head, still coiffed with the tricorne, and to bring it back to Lady H.

On occasion, she would fall for no apparent reason in the middle of the countryside. She would be brought to with a drop of whiskey and would climb back into the saddle and catch up with the rest of the team. One day her mount refused to jump a stream in full flood. We saw Lady H. fly up into the air and disappear, swept away by the current. When she'd been fished out by two or three young strong men, her make-up streaming in her wrinkles, her soaking skirt spread out beneath her, we thought she was going to pass away, vomiting up muddy water and wracked with spasms. An ambulance came for her. No sooner was she lying on the stretcher than she came to and had them drive her back to Kinvara. That very night she offered a glass to her rescuers, having taken the time to make herself up, fix her hair and change into a petrel blue dressing-gown. More of a lady than ever.

Rumour had it that after she had escaped from drowning, she had summoned her solicitor from Galway and dictated her will. One of the clauses specified that after her death her corpse was to be thrown to the hounds.

Something had snapped in her all the same. No one could believe that she was afraid now. It is more likely, I would say, that, having failed to meet her death that day, she waited for it all the more patiently at home, in those dark rooms, which in the evening were coloured with the golden reds of the setting sun.

A little later, at a crossroads we saw her in her old Ford, parked on the roadside, her hands on the wheel, looking amusedly at the cars spinning by. Imagining that the car had broken down and that she was waiting for a mechanic to fall from heaven by some unbidden spell, I drew up next to her, got out and went over to the car door with the window rolled down. It wasn't insensitive to ask her if she needed a hand.

'I'm on my way home', she said. 'The right road doesn't go by here all the time. I have to wait and jump on it when it slows down.'

'Do you want to follow me? It would be easier.'

'I would but the engine won't start.'

She was no longer the same. A sweetness had slipped into her voice, signalling a weakness that was most unlike her. Her impish smile was heart-breaking; she seemed at sea. Turning to C, who was waiting for me in our car, I said that Lady H. couldn't remember the way home to Kinvara. To our great surprise, she interrupted me in French with only the slightest accent.

'But I do, I do know the way. I just want to take a different route.'

She allowed herself to be convinced – and that perhaps was all she wanted without knowing how to express it – and moved to the passenger seat. The Ford started up at once and we headed for Kinvara. C. followed. I stopped in front of Dun Guaire and parked the car.

'Well', she said in a very reassuring tone, 'I really enjoyed our spin. I can't invite you in. I only have one elderly servant in my employ and she is quite soft in the head, very soft indeed.'

WE WERE SPENDING the summer in Greece when Lady H. died in a most discreet fashion. When faced with a mystery, there is nothing better to clear it up than to let your imagination run wild. The will did not stipulate that her body was to be left to the fierce appetite of the pack, which, in any case, would have had only bones to gnaw on. Following her instructions, the woman who tended to her with adoration for years dressed her for the last time in her hunting gear. The most difficult thing of all, apparently, was putting on her boots, which were made by a great craftsman. In full make-up, a smile of complicity still on her lips, her closed eyes demanded silence. Her coffin was nailed outside afterwards, but only when her son, who had travelled from London, had locked the door, turning the enormous key that he gave to a child to throw into Galway Bay. If she had had more imagination, the turning of the key should have set off an enormous explosion that would have set fire to Dun Guaire and been greeted by rapturous applause.

Dun Guaire was turned over to the Irish state, which did with it what we know. The witnesses to that era are growing ever thinner on the ground and those who remain are quick to forget. The silence has grown thicker and no one seems to be concerned to interrupt it.

I NEVER PASS BY Kinvara without remembering the long disjointed silhouette of a woman riding side-saddle and galloping towards the hedges behind the master. I take Félicien Marceau, a summer visitor for years now, to visit the place. We cannot always go to Moran's. From time to time, we have to check that there is nothing better on offer in the region and so we try another place which quickly disappoints us and discourages us from undertaking any new adventures. In the pub-restaurant near the quay, a pretty waitress, whose presence makes us less demanding of the quality of the cooking, is replaced by her mother, a small, curly-haired woman full of provincial goodwill. She harries the undecided clients in an uncouth, authoritarian manner and decides on our menus herself. Félicien and I allow ourselves to be bullied into the 'fish of the day'. In actual fact, the fish of the day is barely defrosted cod, hastily dipped in batter. The Bulgarian white is drinkable. When I ask for the bill, I add: 'Since the fresh fish of the day wasn't defrosted properly, I assume everything is free today.'

Very seriously, clasping her hands together to beg our indulgence, she replies instantly: 'You're out of luck, sir. It's free all week except on Saturday, and God, who thinks of everything, has ensured that today is Saturday.'

She appears to be in such good humour that I ask her about Lady H. She raises her arms to the sky: 'Did we know her? Did we ever! She was a queen. As soon as she arrived in Kinvara everyone was at her beck and call. A word from her and the plumber, the electrician, the roofer, the mason, the carpenter would be up there at a moment's notice. I wonder if any of them dared to ask to be paid. She told her life's story to Dr Powell. It was a secret but when people have gone to heaven, there are no secrets on earth. We no longer belong to ourselves. The doctor told us that in her youth she had been a milliner in London and also in Paris, before marrying an English nobleman, Lord H. It was an unconsummated marriage, but after taking a bath in the same water as her husband, she became pregnant. Even though she was a mother, she was a virgin.'

The case warrants no discussion and is repeated only once every two thousand years ...

ON THE WAY BACK, passing in front of Dun Guaire, I see a huge coach dropping off a pack of tourists, who follow their guide in a downcast fashion. One after the other they pass over the drawbridge and are swallowed up by the castle's postern gate. That happened years ago; I have never seen them come out again.

4.

WE SPENT two winters in the pretentiously named Castle Colgan Country Club, situated on the road between Ardrahan and Ballindereen, a wooded landscape with marshes full of snipe and loughs full of ducks. Far from being a castle, I believe it was a retreat house for nuns. The disaffected chapel served as a garage, and in the bar people hadn't dared, or had forgotten, to remove the crucifix – the Christ-figure on it lowers his head and averts his eyes, lest people might take him for a killjoy in the midst of all the partying. On the first floor, a long corridor, carpeted in psychedelic purple, opened on to five or six bedrooms. On the floor below was a dining-room and a heated swimming pool that only our children made use of. Kilcolgan Park's glory days were long past. Nonetheless, the grounds were home to magnificent oak trees, and to a forest of ash trees and young pines. A trout river flowed in a ring within the property, but I am not an angler. However, there was a promising wooded hill that overlooked several fields, and in the evening flocks of pigeons flew over there to roost. When hidden behind a wall, a good marksman could knock off a couple of birds, thus improving the rather monotonous dinner menu.

Both years at Christmas the hotel staff disappeared for a week. The young cook left us with dishes to heat up or defrost. We changed tables at every meal, leaving the remains of our repast to the mice and the nocturnal cats so that, on their return, the waitresses had to use the dessert-trolley to clear the tables. On Friday and Saturday evenings, the bar was full of a hoard of noisy people who disappeared on the stroke of midnight. The murmuring of the great oaks, harried by the west wind, and the clicking of the slates on the roof replaced the braying voices. In fact, outside the opening hours of the bar, we were the only guests in a low-budget business run in a very amateurish yet completely charming fashion. If I remember correctly, I did a lot of work in a narrow room with a big ugly Victorian table and a large armchair, in which the Mother Superior must have listened to the tales of woe of her supplicants as they examined their consciences. I hunted or simply walked through the countryside, and there I started and finished a novel that bore the imprint of the brown grasses, black loughs, bogs and rocky outcrops (we were close to the granite cliffs of the Burren). I spoke to the neighbouring farmers and would go and sit at the edge of Galway Bay on a strand of grey stones where the seagulls landed in their hundreds.

In the morning the arrival of Tim the postman was one of the highlights of my day. From my window I could see his long silhouette come through the gate of the grounds, pedalling with slow deliberation on his ancient bicycle, covered with a yellow oilskin protecting the handlebars and the weathered leather satchel that contained the mail. As he reached the front porch, he would remove his peaked cap of boiled wool, revealing a helmet of white-hair, cut in a pudding-bowl style. Against the wind, in driving rain, he brought news from the Continent and packages of books. Each time he came, we talked for a while, mostly about hunting. He loved to hunt and had stopped only because of an accident – he had tripped on a root and shot himself in the foot with some pellets. He was a handsome spare man with a network of wrinkles on his face and, although he was heading for his seventieth birthday, he refused to retire, convinced that his daily round, carried out come hail, rain or snow, would keep him in good form forever.

'Anyone who retires before their time signs their own death warrant.'

He had a point. The journey to Ballindereen and back again was a good round trip of twenty miles, a trip broken by frequent stops at farmhouses and cottages along the way.

'The dogs,' he said, 'are my only problem. They go mad when I arrive.'

From ancient times there has been a conflict that opposes postmen and dogs. It must be genetic. Tim was like Prometheus when, standing upright on the pedals, he climbed the slight incline that led to us. In the afternoon he was to be found in the shop-cum-post office in Ballindereen sitting by a turf fire. He was already sorting the following day's letters and imbibing the smell of herrings, stale biscuits and petrol characteristic of his small shop. His big chapped hands put the letters and the packets in order. When he was unsure of an address, he stood up and held the envelope or label closer to the light of the single naked bulb that was covered with fly droppings; it dangled on a dodgy wire from the ceiling, which creaked painfully at every step taken by one of his relatives who was confined to the attic. This was scarcely forty years ago. Now Ballindereen is a cheerful, colourful village, bedecked in pinks and greens; some houses have geraniums in window-boxes and well-tended gardens, and I have difficulty in visualizing the austerity of not so long ago.

During our first winter in Ireland Tim was suddenly replaced by a postman on a motorbike – a sign that modernity would not pass us by. This good-humoured, even jovial young man appeared to take less care with the packets of books and newspapers. He didn't waste any time either on idle chatter about the rain or the occasional appearance of a weak winter sun. When I asked him if Tim had retired or had been taken ill, he replied that he hadn't at all: 'Every two years, at the same time, he goes off on holiday to California, to visit his daughter, who has a hair salon in San Francisco.'

It was hard to imagine Tim going from his antique bike to a supersonic jumbo jet, wearing his big postman's cap and trussed up in his black Sunday suit, with his trouser legs stuffed into his bicycle-clips to reveal huge clodhopper shoes, and then landing in Frisco in the pleasant light of a city so bright and so gay. What would people think of him when they saw him in the streets of Chinatown or Fisherman's Wharf, that is, if they looked at him at all, because the city of San Francisco is so explosively original itself that its numerous eccentrics go unnoticed. So this big Irishman, with his thin rangy body, his cheeks made rosy by the cold, the hail and the icy rain, and his blue eyes that were beginning to cloud over with the trace of a ripening cataract, Tim from Ballindereen, could be taken for an actor who had escaped from a set or from the rehearsals of *The Playboy of the Western World* or *The Plough and the Stars*.

On the day he returned to work, there was one of those torrential and incessant downpours that flood everything in their path. The water creeps into even the most waterproof of homes, and the air one breathes is so humid that you'd think you were in an aquarium, even if, two hours later, the countryside is inundated with radiant sunshine. Tim could have waited before setting off on the road but I suppose that after his weeks of enforced rest, he was afraid of being rusty, of breaking the routine to which he'd been attached for years. When he entered the grounds, I could see from his hunched figure and from the zigzags of his bicycle that he was under strain, as he rarely had been before, and gritting his teeth. Was he cursing his beloved old Ireland, which was being whipped by the elements as if it had been sinning since the creation of the world? Tim kept smiling and opened his oilskin that protected the day's messages.

'How did you get on in San Francisco, Tim?'

'My daughter wants me to go and live with her in her pretty house with a swimming pool. She's really a good girl and her children are beautiful, but that city with all its ups and downs, and crowds and noise and sunshine and eathquakes – none of that is a patch on Ballindereen.'

And since then, every time I pass through Ballindereen I think of Tim who preferred his native village to San Francisco. Would he have liked the changes in his country? The painted or whitewashed houses, the abundance of geraniums, the tidily kept gardens, the rented cars that whizz through the village bearing tourists to Kinvara or Ballyvaughan, the drying up of the bogland? Would he shed a tear in memory of the poky little shop-cum-post office, the road that flooded under the slightest downpour, the freezing church, and the petrol pump that the shopkeeper manoeuvred with a fierce energy one could only dream of?

5.

IT IS IMPOSSIBLE to refer to Tim without talking about
Patrick-Joseph Smith, whom ever since our arrival in Tynagh
we called Pat-Jo, as was the local custom. Like the postman
from Ballindereen, he was a tall, lean man with hollow cheeks.
His face was shaven, but badly, leaving tufts of growth here
and there; he had an aquiline nose, reddish skin, and a wide
wrinkled forehead under a shock of unruly white hair. I called
him old Pat-Jo until I found out that he was ten years younger
than me. He was supposed to be one of the last dry-stone wall
builders, the infamous hunger walls that have cut the west of
Ireland into a patchwork of lace. And it is true that repairing
those walls made of large stones collected in the fields where
they appear to grow like weeds is an art.

Pat-Jo appeared one morning in a three-piece suit – let's call it crumpled so as to spare his shade's blushes, as he is always with us in spirit – a check shirt, a soft grey felt hat with a broad ring of sweat around it instead of a ribbon, and huge canvas boots knotted with pieces of twine. He was driving a tractor, and every time it backfired we expected it to explode and spread the remains of its bodywork and engine parts along the road. A sheepdog – a mongrel rough collie – was standing in the trailer behind; he jumped off as soon as it stopped to go back to his master's side. A man who is loved by his dog cannot be all bad.

At work Pat-Jo took his time, but by the end of the day he had finished a section of wall, planted a reasonable number of stakes for an enclosure or repaired a roof, without stopping except to plug his pipe with black tarry tobacco. He would pull a block of compressed tobacco from his pocket and, with the help of his pocket-knife, would cut off fine strips and push them into the bowl with his thumb. The other hand, which was missing the index finger because it had been cut off one day in a sawmill, lit a gas-fired lighter, which produced a flame worthy of a blowtorch. Although he was taciturn during the first few days, he soon felt at home with these strangers from another planet, and we discovered his sharp cleverness, an intelligence far superior to than what his rugged appearance betrayed. He was a free spirit, capable of disappearing for a week and then returning unexpectedly, as if nothing had happened. We had the loosest of contracts: he appeared, disappeared and started up again without a word, always at the same pace, indifferent to wind and rain, and to solitude if we could find no one to help him. On sunny days he kept his grey hat on but removed his jacket and shirt to bring in the hay or the straw, bare-chested under his braces. Time and time again I thought about taking his photo. He wouldn't have minded, but fixing his image on paper in that way made me uneasy for reasons linked to the respect he inspired in me.

Sometimes, after an over-long absence that had begun to worry us, I would go out to his place in Duniry. His door remained open day and night. It was situated at the edge of a country lane next to some meadows and not far from a trout fishing stream, and on the other side of the track, under an awning, was a pile of bric-a-brac that he had been collecting over the centuries – old carts, harrows, barrels of diesel, broken fuel tanks, dislocated tractors, piles of useless tyres and a forge with a huge pair of long-unused bellows. Pat-Jo still loved to potter around, and he made us a grill, jumps and gates, all wrought of ugly scrap metal, sculptures like those of Tanguy, but less boring and which barely outlived him.

I would knock at the glass door, get no response, and end up by going inside into a dark hallway that led to two rooms. Down at the end was the kitchen – if 'kitchen' isn't too elaborate a term for a room containing one cupboard whose broken doors revealed a couple of damaged implements, and, abandoned on a table covered with an oilcloth, a chipped bowl, some cereal boxes, and a frying pan in which he must have cooked rashers and eggs from time to time. At the sound of my footsteps, he would appear in a nightshirt already wearing his canvas boots.

'Wait a minute,' he would say, running his mutilated hand through his straight hair.

I would hear the gurgling of a water tank under the roof. Every morning he showered carefully in cold water and clad himself again in his ever-present business and leisure suit that mixed an honest smell of dirt with a doubtful fragrance of soap. In the kitchen, while he gulped down his bowl of cereal with the milk he got from one of his cows, we exchanged a few jokes about the changeable weather and the newspaper headlines of the previous day's paper that I had brought him: it could have been dated from the previous year and it wouldn't have changed his disillusioned comments. Although his preference was for Fianna Fáil, the Soldiers of Destiny, he no longer voted; he was too sceptical to encourage any party. One day I opened a tabloid that always had a scantily clad actress or model on page 3, and I saw him looking at the pretty girl.

'Pat-Jo, did you ever feel like getting married?'

No, because the opportunity had never arisen. Although he was over fifty, he had never been in love.

'There is time enough for that kind of thing,' he said without regret, leaving the door open for a faint hope.

It took me a while to find out that when he didn't work for us he spent hours filling out the tax returns or doing the accounts for his neighbours, and preparing their plans for a stable or a barn. Had he been born elsewhere ('I was one of ten children and, until the age of twelve when I left school to help my father, we never had anything other than cold water and potatoes to live on; my mother, sitting in her wheelchair, would prepare the potatoes in a basin of water, and cooked them over the fire. I only ever saw her in a wheelchair and heavy with the six kids born after me '), he would have become an architect, an engineer or an entrepreneur without being any the happier. He was Diogenes but without the whole joke of the barrel and the lamp, without the pretension of the philosopher, happy with his daily bread and giving no thought to the superfluous. His naturally noble and reserved nature, the flicker of devilment that shone in his eyes when he found something funny, forbade all questions.

In the beginning, when our relationship was still episodic, he would go off to a widow's house where they would share unvarying meals of cabbage and bacon and tea and biscuits. When she was hospitalized, he agreed to have lunch with us, taking off his hat and putting on his jacket before, after or during the meal. He liked to stick with what he knew. I admired the very Irish privilege of being at ease everywhere, being uncomfortable in no situation, an exemplary absence of barriers between people, a social fabric with no class divisions.

Two of Pat-Jo's sisters were members of an enclosed order and the idea of going to visit them never entered his head. One of his brothers lived in England and never wrote to him. And as for the others? They were not endowed with a healthy constitution ... And for a while now he himself hadn't been in very good shape. He had sore feet and had to wear several pairs of socks to be able to walk. We encouraged him to see a doctor. He came back from the consultation a bit stunned and almost proud.

'I have leprosy,' he said. 'There's no cure for it.'

'There's no cure but the progression of the disease can be slowed down.'

He didn't seem too sure and a few days later came back with a return ticket for Lourdes.

'In any case, I've been wanting to go there for a long time.'

He had never left Ireland before (perhaps he had never left County Galway), nor taken a plane. This didn't daunt him. Under the protection of St Bernadette and the Virgin Mary, the voyage seemed very promising. In fact, he came back a week later beaming with joy. He had replaced his canvas boots with new leather ones; they were still very big but he walked without grimacing. After soaking his feet in holy water while he recited the rosary, his scaly scabs disappeared. The leprosy had disappeared, or at least the diagnosis of it by a country doctor. With a group of adventurous Irish tourists, mostly priests and nuns, he had even crossed the Spanish border in a coach. This brief experience of foreign lands left him with mixed feelings, but a couple of months later when our son asked him to go to Paris to help him fix up the house he had bought, Pat-Jo put on his Sunday suit and packed his bag. We met him in Paris after finishing work one Sunday and he came out to lunch with us in Les Ministères restaurant on the rue du Bac. He was unchanged, very much at ease, not at all shy of French cuisine and happy to work for Alexandre in the house he was helping him renovate, complaining only of the noise of the traffic which meant that he couldn't sleep with the window open. Alexandre had taken the time to accompany him to the Eiffel Tower and the Louvre; he also took him down the Champs Elysées, but none of these things had filled him with wonder. I expected him to say: 'None of these places come close to Duniry', but he didn't; he went back to his icy cold house, his old wood-burning oven, his worn-out fields, his few cows, and to us, who from then on he saw as family, not that he gave any excessive demonstrations of affection.

WE HAD the first sign of trouble one morning when I went to find him. As usual, all the doors were open; the cereal was on the kitchen table with a half-drunk cup of tea. The neighbour told me that an ambulance had come to take Pat-Jo to the regional hospital the previous day. Finding him there was no small task in the disorder of the different units, an atrocious dive into human suffering displayed for all to see through lack of space. When I did locate him in a ward with a dozen other patients, after coming across several Smiths who were not mine, he winked at me and, with a bob of his chin, indicated the curtains pulled around another bed. The fellow over there was gone but Pat-Jo himself was still there, alive and even, it seemed to me, in excellent form, despite being forbidden to smoke his pipe in bed. He kept it under his pillow and showed me how he could draw on it a few times by putting the sheet over his head and pretending to be asleep. The only problem was the lack of tobacco – a problem I soon solved. What had happened to him? A sudden weakness, a bout of vomiting and a short spell in a coma, of which he remembered nothing. He was being kept in for observation and was anxious to get back to Duniry. He was lucky; they found nothing wrong that time round. The doctor thought it was the result of a bad hangover after drinking too much beer. Pat-Jo used to go out drinking sometimes, only on Saturday night, and he admitted that the following day after a dozen pints he didn't feel that well. Better than in hospital, though, where you couldn't smoke without setting off the fire alarm and the cries of the head nurse, here known as matron, a word that comes from old French and is often inadequate, since the nurses in Irish hospitals are very nice to look at, particularly in their flimsy nylon uniforms.

He escaped. There is no other word for it, and no other explanation either. How he managed to find his clothes, and how he got home without alerting anybody, I don't know. There was no investigation; the overcrowded hospital, with patients waiting for days on stretchers in the corridors, was not going to put out a missing persons alert.

When I heard about it, I found him at home fresh-faced and smiling as if he had played a practical joke; he was in better shape because of a more moderate diet. However, things did not return to normal. He hardly ever left his house. The neighbour looked after his few cows. One morning I called in to bring him out for lunch; he had prepared a present wrapped up in newspaper.

'I have two books, but the print is too small for my eyes. Alice will surely enjoy them; she loves books like you do.'

We still have the two bound volumes of the *Cyclopaedia of English Literature* published by Robert Chambers, Edinburgh

1844, and I often consult the pages devoted to the eighteenth century, a rich period for English literature. How did this learned volume, with its detailed information (notably on Chaucer, Sterne and Tobias Smollett), end up at Pat-Jo's place and, what's more, in relatively good condition?

'When I was younger', he said, 'I bought it from a travelling salesman because it interested me, but I haven't had time to read it all. There are too many verses in it and I don't understand poetry.'

Pat-Jo hoisted no more than a corner of the sail. He detached himself slowly from everything, without losing any of his good humour. His gaze was already drawn towards a faraway horizon, but perhaps I am interpreting signs that became clear to me only after his death. Sometimes, he confided in me with glee:

'One glorious day, I shall be reunited with my family. My mother, without her wheelchair; she will be cured. My brothers, my sisters, all of us will finally be together. They will be very happy to see me, to touch me to be sure that it is true and that I was the one in the family who was miraculously healed because of the Virgin Mary and Saint Bernadette. When you're sure of that, nothing else is important.'

He didn't have to wait long. A few days later my wife and I went to the regional hospital. It was already too late. A carer took his face in her hands and shook him.

'Hello, Patrick-Joseph, your friends are here.'

His eyelids lifted; he stared blindly at us and then closed his eyes again. He passed away that same night.

AS HE WAS LOWERED into his grave at Tynagh Cemetery, I repeated the last words he said to me. If he was with his family at that moment, as he believed he would be, he must have been jumping for joy. If he wasn't, a special grace had lit up his final days on earth.

Over half a century of international organized crime and social upheaval, Pat-Jo had experienced only minor troubles, and had borne them with an indulgent smile. As for the world's great, incurable problems that humanity will always suffer from, he left them for other people to worry over. His 'miraculous' healing at Lourdes did not make him any more devout. How could he have been grateful to God for His kind deed, when God is the Almighty? Nothing is difficult for Him: He can appease man's suffering in the blink of an eye. Life's woes are there so that on the day of Glory His creatures will know true bliss.

If we had been in France, I would have liked to accompany the last glimpse of his coffin with a few words by Chateaubriand: 'Old Age is a night-time traveller: the earth is hidden from view, now only the heavens she sees.'

6.

I AM NOT the only one to have witnessed the brief return of a
ghost from heaven – the faithful people of Tynagh can bear
out my story. Our parish priest, Father Campbell, had just died.
I cannot claim to have known him very well but he had been
good to us, and this former teacher of history and geography
at a secondary school in Ballinasloe was a cultured man. We
were not among his most assiduous churchgoers, except for
the funerals or weddings of friends. He never dared to ask
about the faith of the French couple and their two children, but
from time to time, on sunny days, on his way back from the
neighbouring school after a catechism class, he would pay us
a short visit and talk about this and that, refuse the obligatory
cup of tea, admire the garden and leave again, walking gently

with his hands clasped behind his back. He was not part of the new Catholicism: he was always dressed in a black suit with a dog collar, his short grey hair carefully combed; he had an intelligent, thoughtful face, and unwavering inner calm. No one in high places had thought of him for a diocesan position; seeing out his days in this large rural parish with its modest, unproblematic inhabitants did not do justice to this good man. Such hierarchical inequality when you consider his bishop, Eamonn Casey, a shamelessly cynical crook! Father Campbell accepted the sacrifice imposed by his superiors without anger or bitterness.

We regretted his death, and his discreet visitations that only ever amounted to a banal exchange of pleasantries, always putting off more personal conversations until a later date. In response to my offer to lend him some books, he had assured me that he had enough of them to occupy his evenings in the presbytery. He only read books in English and in Latin. In Latin I did have a copy of *The Art of Love* and *The Remedies for Love* by Ovid, or the love poems of Catullus. He did not say *Vade retro!* to me, but I understood that those works were not his field of interest.

He died discreetly in hospital – so discreetly that we were unaware of his hospitalization. He spared us the lugubrious and traditional viewing of the corpse – hands joined, reddened lips and cheeks, nose bedecked with glasses (to see what, in the eternal night?).

The hearse was going to unload the coffin outside the new church. I write 'new' because we live in the old presbytery and use the former church, now deconsecrated, for domestic use, as a storage space. From the outside the new parish church looks more like a hammam or a sporting complex. However, it does have the advantage of being closer to the village and is endowed with a car park and central heating, modern amenities that ensure a minimum level of comfort, useful for the maintenance of the rites of faith.

There is no organ. The harmonium is played by a young nun from a religious community in Athlone: well-built with flame-coloured cheeks, she is the image of gaiety itself. She is the youngest daughter in a family in which each member is so gifted with a different musical instrument that they could form a symphony orchestra by themselves. Sister M. has put together a choir with the boys and girls from the village and the surrounding areas, who can easily sing a Bach Cantata to a pop rhythm.

We were guided to the front row, not out of deference to foreigners but because of an error – we had arrived early. The church building did not inspire silence. If from the outside it resembled a sports complex, from the inside it had more in common with a refectory. People murmured, coughed, turned round repeatedly to see who was present and absent. The children couldn't stay still, they asked naïve questions in loud voices and their parents made even more noise than them trying to get them to keep quiet.

At last, almost on time, four strong men showed up bearing the coffin. Dressed for a wedding, the men, focused by the importance of their mission, their faces reddened by the effort and by the preliminaries in the pub, walked down the central aisle and placed their burden at the foot of the altar. It occurred to me that if Father Campbell still had any communication with this world, he would have been moved to see the church then, although he probably hadn't liked very much while he was alive. It was the image of the final years of his sacrificial sacred ministry. Won't we all end up one day missing the things we were indifferent to in happier times past? No one would have been surprised if Father Campbell had suddenly started thumping the inside of his fake oak prison and ordered the undertakers to unscrew the coffin and let him have one last look to make sure that everything was in its place – the lilies, the wine cruet, the missal. But no, that time was past. Inside the coffin, death had already started its slow work of decomposition.

It was at that moment, when we were all probably trying to conjure up our own memories of him, that Father Campbell appeared in his priestly habit, hands joined, murmuring an inaudible prayer. Two altar boys and a novice were following him.

Everything that runs through your head when faced with such a completely unreal incident is so chaotic, so troubled – especially years later when you're trying to remember what you were thinking, and you're not sure if your memory has muddled the details – that you can't very well describe what you felt. I must have fallen victim to one of those collective hallucinations that take hold of the most disparate of gatherings. I hadn't been drinking, I wasn't dreaming. I was in a totally normal state; my wife, at my side, was not at all surprised by what was happening – I was going to say on stage – no I mean in front of the altar, where Father Campbell was both imprisoned in the bier and upright, turned towards the congregation and himself, making a sign of the cross in the air where several wisps of incense floated. Nobody at that moment could deny the priest's double presence – one was distressing, the other perfectly serene. In writing 'nobody could deny' I am not taking too many risks because I didn't even think of turning around. In all logic, some ladies should have fainted and two or three men should have stood up and thrown the celebrant roughly out of the church, like a troublemaker out of a pub. Or, was I, along with the others present, yielding to the call of the supernatural so true to the Irish imagination and indulging in some phenomenon of the transmigration of the soul or an improbable resurrection – ideas that my poor agnosticism refused categorically to entertain, in spite of the evidence. In this century of unbelievers, whether one was a believer or at least, in the words of Pascal, a doubter, one had the right to wonder why the God of the Christians had awakened Father Campbell who was sleeping so peacefully amongst the blessed. So that he could say his own funeral mass? So that he could remind the living that death is also a beatitude, that Paradise is but a delicious pause, *lux, pax et refrigerium*, before the great Resurrection?

The more I looked at Father Campbell celebrating his own funeral mass, the more I recognized his gestures, his voice and, at the very moment of the elevation of the host, his disregard for vanity. Paralyzed by these conclusions, with my throat constricted to the point of not being able to talk to C, for whom this completely unexpected resurrection, which was enough to shake the most profound agnostic, seemed perfectly natural, I felt isolated by the absolute confidence of the believers around me. I gave in to the reflex that still dogs me today – although to a much lesser extent – my hand dug into my pocket to take out my box of cigarillos, my remedy for writer's block. Had C. not slapped the back of my hand, I think I would have lit one. The box fell and the little Davidoff rolled under the benches. The nuisance and the stupidity of my reflex action, or the annoyance of not daring to go down on all fours to retrieve the precious cigarillos brought back from Paris and impossible to find in Ireland, must have jolted me back to earth, to this earth and to the mercy of the ancient magicians of the Catholic Church.

In the end, a plausible explanation came to mind – I must have misheard the name of the person we were burying. It wasn't Father Campbell but one of our fellow parishioners whose name also ended in 'bell'. Our wonderful priest was still alive, and I felt like hugging him and telling him how sorry I had been for the mix-up. The man he was readying for eternity must have been a close relative because repeatedly, when he turned in our direction, his eyes welled up with tears. Marrying, baptizing and administering extreme unction must harden a priest, but despite his cold exterior, Father Campbell was – as we all guessed – a sensitive man. The hypothesis seemed quite simple – I had witnessed a miracle. God gets tired of bigots who lay siege to him pitilessly for minor details. From time to time, he cynically likes to provoke some confusion among them by sending someone (one of the elect of course) to help another chosen one in his final meeting with the world of men. The case was no doubt rare, but whose soul was Father Campbell helping to entrust to God?

I heard the answer in the crush of the crowd, which surrounded the hearse ready to take the coffin on its last journey. The four brutes were already loading it. The excitement of this strange ceremony was due to the fact that the priest on the altar was indeed Father Campbell, not our priest, but his twin brother, who had been ordained to the priesthood on the same day as him, fifty years earlier. The discipline of their calling had maintained a close resemblance between them. I was the only one in the dark. The confusion did prompt me to return to the writings of Philippe Ariès on death and to a history of Paradise, which has had such an important place in the Celtic imagination since Christ showed Saint Patrick the obscure hole where those who spend a day and a night are cleansed of their sins before ascending to the realm of the blessed. Was not our dear Pat-Jo convinced of this?

Far from stifling the imagination, faith throws its gates wide open, consoling mourners who still tread this earth impatiently. Our friends the Ks who live in County Wicklow lost their son Richie. The family had bred horses for generations. Richie had taken over the stud farm from his father. He was a handsome man, gentle and hardworking, passionate about his job. A kick from a stallion killed him stone dead. The distraught Ks left their home and travelled to visit their friends scattered between

Wicklow and Galway. Knowing that words of condolence are more heart-rending than consoling, over lunch I said to Mrs K, 'Richie will have certainly found some horse to break in and ride, up there.'

Mrs K's kindly face lit up.

'Oh, yes. If he hadn't he would have already come back to us.'

This admirable form of consolation is the greatest fruit of a Christian education. A zest of Irish humour suppressing the very thought of a tear.

UNFORTUNATELY, it happens that the servants of God may sometimes dramatically abuse the confidence accorded to them because of their function. This was the case with Father Sean Fortune, a priest in New Ross, County Wicklow. I have before my eyes a cutting from *The Irish Times* with a photograph of the scoundrel. The article is by Alison O'Connor, who in 2000 published *A Message from Heaven – The Life and Crimes of Father Sean Fortune*. The photo alone is almost enough to condemn the priest: his face is swollen and flabby, his mouth is thin with no lips, his enormous neck goes right up to the tip of his chin, spilling over his collar at the back in rolls of fat; his small, tinted glasses make him look like he's pretending to be blind, and hide a pair of undisputably piggy eyes. His housekeeper must have placed a pudding bowl on his whale of a head and cut his stiff liquorice-like hair. This hippopotamus is not a joyous Rabelaisian monk, protector of the poor and oppressed, fighter against folly; he is a monster of lust and lucre, an unrepentant paedophile, an alcoholic who helped himself to the donations of the faithful with repulsive dishonesty. He was lucky to have a worldly bishop in the figure of Brendan Comiskey, who was consumed with bitterness at having gained no prestige after being appointed to a diocese. Was this the reason for this prelate's addiction to the demon drink and his trips abroad to dry out? In truth, he was a weak, influenceable soul, manipulated by a clever pervert.

When the complaints from the parents of Father Fortune's victims began to accumulate, Bishop Comiskey had to hand them over to the police. There were sixty-six of them in all! Only one six short of being the work of the devil. During his first court appearance, Father Fortune emphatically denied everything. It was too late; the witness testimonies left no room for any doubt. He could perjure himself, lie to the judge, to the police, lie to himself with so much conviction that he believed it himself. But the truth, with all its terrible catastrophic consequences for Ireland's clergy, burst forth. When he got home, he said he was going on a trip and gave his housekeeper and gardener two days off.

On a cold March night in 1999, the monster shut himself up in the presbytery and pulled down the blinds. A box of sleeping tablets and half a bottle of whiskey ended a life of incredible wrongdoing and barefaced lies. The whiskey gave him energy for the long journey that awaited him: one for the road, as they say in Ireland.

The housekeeper and the gardener found him lying on his bed, rosary beads in his joined hands and a breviary open next to him. What was the page? The enquiry remained silent on that count. On his bedside table there was a poem:

From Paradise
To my family, to be read at my Requiem Mass

In a note, he accused the press of slander and said he preferred to leave for a better place.

Once again he had cheated his accusers and deprived his victims of finally hearing the truth that would confound him.

While he paid with his life for the grotesque setting and self-righteous message, did he really believe that his death would dissipate any doubts as to his guilt in the face of his disdainful denials? In declaring Paradise as his new address, he pre-empted the judgment of God and dispensed himself from any time in the dark hole revealed by Jesus to Saint Patrick. Father Fortune, who had experienced Purgatory on earth, had placed himself on the right hand of God. Even in the hereafter he remained diabolical – like Nero reciting his prayers while the Irish Catholic Church, to which he had set fire, burned.

7.

THERE ARE BARELY a dozen of us in a private drawing-room in
the Shelbourne Hotel on St Stephen's Green. With the exception of a journalist from the *Irish Independent*, who had come
to interview me in the west and had produced a slightly patro-
nizing article, and Christopher Sinclair-Stevenson, publisher at
Hamish Hamilton, I know no one. I have come from Galway
and am leaving again the following day to spend a few days in
Paris. Christopher arrived from London in the afternoon with
the intention, I suppose, of proving to us that God exists, that
he is publishing us and doesn't disdain from taking a fatherly
interest in us. All the present company have published a book
this year. There is a table laden with a buffet of snacks, Jameson,
and even a carafe of orangeade, in the unlikely case that some

of us might abstain from alcohol – *teetotal* is the word I believe. Christopher is standing behind the buffet and is encouraging us to help ourselves. He needn't have bothered: everyone already has a glass in hand, certainly not their first, and I will find it difficult to catch up after the time I spent driving around in the rain and the swiftly fallen darkness. The voices indicate that the conversations have already gone up an octave.

The assembly is very varied. I don't mean that it is simply divided between fat and thin, short and tall, bearded and clean-shaven, but more that people are dressed differently, from country-style corduroys and urban jeans to the full three-piece suit of the city-dwelling bureaucrat. The biggest difference can be seen in the two groups that have formed away from each other. It is easy to identify them by their accents: on one side there are the English – or, so as not to offend anyone, the British (Brits) – from Ulster or London, on the other side the Irish from the south or the west. They resemble two rugby teams having a confab before the match starts. If Christopher's idea was to break the ice, I fear he was not very successful. Christopher Sinclair-Stevenson, our publisher, protected by the buffet table, perfectly turned out in his grey Savile Row suit, with a very blue shirt and a grey silk tie, is the only common denominator between us (authors rarely read each others' work – 'When you start to write, you stop reading,' as Chateaubriand used to say).

Christopher had no need to blow the whistle to start the match. I had just exchanged a couple of words with him when a furious voice rose above the hum.

'I'm going to kick that hoor of an Englishman up the arse, if he doesn't leave this instant. What is he doing in my country?'

'Ulick, Ulick, please!' Christopher implored.

A bearded man in an Aran sweater with dishevelled hair headed out the door without a word. The first man, with the Scandinavian name of Ulick, was of average height, wearing a navy blue blazer with several layers of dandruff on his shoulders, a pair of shabby grey trousers and runners; his shirt was impeccable, though bright orange and worn with a bronze-coloured tie. The confusion in his vestimentary habits aside, the man was handsome, no doubt about it: he looked very good for fifty, and had fine features – a perfect nose was set in his livid face, the nostrils pink and flaring with anger. His grey hair, artistically waved and parted over the right ear to flatten it in the direction of the left one, probably to hide a bald patch, framed a large, noble forehead. The object of his ire had disappeared and Ulick O'Connor, the man in question, turned in my direction.

'The English,' he said in a disillusioned voice, 'as soon as you speak a little louder than them, they run away like rabbits ...'

All this was not very friendly towards Christopher, who had regained his normal colour and, coming out from behind the protective cover of the buffet table, introduced us to each other.

'That guy,' said Ulick, paying no attention to our publisher, 'has just come to live in Ireland to write his crap and to benefit from the tax advantages for artists put in place by Charlie Haughey. I wish that crypto-Marxist could at least shut his mouth when we're talking politics here.'

His anger dissipated when Christopher repeated my name. 'Ah,' he said. 'I go to Paris every year for my holidays. I escape Dublin for a whole week. Christmas is dead here. Everything is closed. I read the article in the *Independent* about you! You should be more careful and ask to reread the interviews. Irish critics are only interested in criticizing the people they interview and when there is no one left to demolish, they self-destruct.'

No matter how often I repeated that the article was rather friendly, apart from a couple of well-judged and perhaps justified digs, Ulick didn't listen. When I told him that I saw him on *The Late, Late Show*, Gay Byrne's programme that explains so much about Ireland, he was surprised.

'That's all over now. Gay fired me for no reason at the end of the season after saying to me on the last evening, "I had forgotten how marvellous you could be. Bye ..."'

Even though I am hardly a faithful television viewer, I was surprised to see him disappear from a programme so characteristic of the Irish 'gift of the gab', but the thing that captivates me most of all about Ulick O'Connor is his talent as a biographer. After reading his *Oliver St John Gogarty*, I finished his biography of Brendan Behan. The astonishing thing in both these books is the talent the intellectual elite in Ireland deploy to raise the minor incidents of life to the level of a Greek tragedy. But when I mentioned this he was troubled, and thought about it, taking an interest in his own case.

'I'm not like that!'

I wasn't so sure, but we would never get to know each other if we each continued to hold such explosive views. The furiously angry man of three minutes previously, who had got rid of a foreign writer, had now turned into to an extremely courteous individual asking for a few seconds of reflection before responding. I seemed to be entering into dangerous territory and, as he was concentrating so hard, with his eyes lowered and his lips barely moving, I asked him: 'You wouldn't be a ventriloquist would you?'

He looks at me in stupefaction.

'How did you know?'

Our intuitions run through us like bolts of lightning and a minute later, despite their violence, disappear, both unexplained and inexplicable. I had no doubt touched on a sensitive subject. He really was a ventriloquist. And also a magician, but he was prouder of having been a lawyer, defender of the oppressed and the defamed. To his CV he boastfully added: 'Ventriloquist, magician, All-Ireland Pole Vaulting Champion and boxer!'

This information I also knew. Christopher, delighted that the ice had been broken, put on his publisher's hat: 'Michel has just published a novel, wonderfully translated by Julian Evans: *Where are you dying tonight?* The title comes from the *Diaries of Evelyn Waugh.*'

'Waugh talks about me in his *Diaries*,' said Ulick, bringing the conversation straight back to himself. 'In 1956, my father and I had dinner with him in the Kildare Street Club. He wrote 'a Professor of Surgery and his son, a boxing lawyer'. The editor of the *Diaries of Evelyn Waugh* is a friend of mine, Michael Davie.'

Christopher felt reassured. As soon as Ulick started name-dropping, high good humour was restored. It is true that in the following thirty minutes, and at dinner, because we stuck together until closing time at a ghastly dive of an Italian restaurant that Ulick dragged me to, promising me the best spaghetti in the world, Ulick was seduction incarnate.

'You know,' he said, 'I might be the world-record man for first round knockouts since the 1950s? In 1980 I went three crazy rounds with Charlie Nash in the warm-up for his fight with Jimmy Watt for the lightweight championship.'

Christopher was not terribly keen on boxing and tried to steer the conversation towards more literary topics, even though I was listing all the writers who liked boxing: Hemingway, Jean Prévost, Maeterlinck, Norman Mailer, Pierre Bessand-Massenet, the distinguished historian, Morand, who perhaps didn't box much but who spoke very well about it in *Champions du Monde*.

Ulick went back to his famous knock-out.

'Four seconds after the bell. On the canvas for the count. An impeccable right. The best of my life.'

He brandished his closed fist under Christopher's nose. Christopher didn't bat an eyelid and returned to his topic.

'Ulick wrote *A Celtic Dawn: A Portrait of the Irish Literary Renaissance*. Michel, you must read it. I've brought a copy for you.'

Yes, of course I'd read it over the coming days and would try to get a French publisher interested in it.

A promise made with no illusions of delivery. The directors of literary collections are proud guardians of their domains.

But how could I explain this to an impetuous Irishman?

'I'm translating Baudelaire,' he said.

'All of Baudelaire?'

'No, a selection: the poems of the damned.'

The strange thing is that he doesn't speak French (or so little for it to make no difference) and that in quoting a verse, or even two lines, his terrible accent made them incomprehensible, but there are such miracles: Giono hardly knew any English and his translation of *Moby-Dick* is blissful.

Ulick was unconcerned by his ignorance of the French language and I didn't risk hinting at it when, having bid farewell to Christopher, we headed for the foul trattoria where he said he was a regular. I spent a good hour listening to him. He sent the spaghetti back twice, the first time because it was too hot, and the second because it was not hot enough. The waiter was used to this, and, because Ulick was sitting with his back to the hatch, I could see the smirking face of the chef who simply made a sign of the cross over the dish each time before sending it back again. The supposed Chianti was undrinkable. Ulick wasn't fussed about such details and found the plonk excellent. He was concentrating on what he was saying and pushed away the trivia of the world with the back of his hand, had no hesitation in cutting his spaghetti with a knife and let half of it fall on the paper tablecloth, when it wasn't on his tie and waistcoat.

I have rarely met someone who radiated such charm and was such a persuasive speaker, but I didn't quite get all the arguments when Ulick moved on to the thorny topic of Ulster, a subject I have always avoided.

He spoke with his lips barely moving, his face half-closed. At the neighbouring table, the conversation had halted. People were listening to him without showing it; I was unsure what lay behind such an ambiguous attitude. In fact, the attention came from unadulterated interest in the conversation itself, and when we stood to leave – I drunk on his words, he swaying no doubt because I'd left him to finish all the fake chianti, then in the fresh air drawing himself up to walk with a hunter's step – when we stood up, the people at the neighbouring table asked for an autograph, which he found particularly flattering in my presence.

On St Stephen's Green, in front of the Shelbourne where two taxis were waiting, the consequences of Ulick's recent choleric outbursts were suddenly obvious. The drivers locked the doors and put up their windows. If I understand what followed correctly, he was not very sure of being accepted by the few buses that were still running and could bring him close to Fairfield Park. So I had to drive him home and drop him off in a cul de sac, where he insisted that I drive him to his front door. On the way back, disorientated in that deserted district, lit only by a few rays of light filtering out of the covered windows of the houses, I began to get lost before finding the canal. By driving along the bank I worked out how to get back to Merrion Square and, to my relief, St Stephen's Green.

In my room, with the curtains pulled back, I open the window: the sky above the psychedelic Temple Bar district is lit up in tints of pink and yellow; the rest of Dublin is extraordinarily calm. The city yields to the night, folded in upon itself, neither hostile nor friendly but different with its dark mysteries, its crumbling memories and perhaps the reflex of guilt that has haunted it since it recovered its freedom after being so cruel to its writers, artists and heroes. Shaw and Joyce left. Wilde and Beckett found peace in Paris, Yeats in Roquebrune. Everything that mattered and still matters today is made great in London, New York or France. The man I'd just left in front of his house in Fairfield Park, Rathgar, proudly stands up to the coteries and the jealousies and pays a heavy price for it. He is Braveheart in the confines of the Celtic lands.

We were, of course, destined to meet again and to forge a real if episodic friendship, interspersed with short curt spaces caused by an awkward word or simply because his visit to Tynagh would have disturbed my work, during which, selfishly, I lock myself away.

In our far-west Irish retreat his coming always leaves a mixed impression. No one could fail to be impressed by his moral standards, his hard-hitting intelligence, and his rich poetic memory. He arrives in the garb of a city-dweller, elegant after his own fashion, that is to say a mixture of a dandy and a tramp – with his clothes half-ragged, half-chic – a large felt hat pulled down over one ear, and a purple cashmere scarf hiding part of the collar of the much-worn black overcoat whose mix and match buttons I can imagine him choosing just to add to the composition of his character. Isn't he already a character? No, I think he just has an aristocratic disdain for the distasteful tasks of everyday life that bore him stiff.

As for housework, that's the privilege of his slaves – he wouldn't dream of depriving them of the joy of preparing the meals, fixing the beds, sweeping, tidying up his worktable, even sacrificing their life for the well-being of their Prince. Ulick is full of surprises, and we were astonished to hear him referring to his father as 'Daddy' and to his mother as 'Mammy', or to hear him reciting a poem for his nanny who looked after him until he was five. Much later, when she was ninety, he remembers taking her to visit the church where she used to take him when he was a child:

> *On your way out*
> *I glanced at the organ loft*
> *Where Joyce's father met his wife*
> *And thought of that devious poet,*
>
> *But was careful not to mention it,*
> *Even in a passing phrase,*
> *For I knew you always thought him responsible*
> *For most of my awkward ways.*

When we first met, he reminded me of Montherlant's *Célibataires*, but while those déclassé gentlemen lead a wretched, dead end existence, Ulick remains the knight of a cause that has lost its integrity over time and allowed itself to be overrun by the violence and crime, always quick to use political debate to spread mafia-like networks of influence throughout Ulster, and even the Republic as a whole.

This is such a delicate subject that I never broach it with him; we never talk about it. The topic creates a no man's land between us, which, as a foreigner, on account of a fatality intrinsic to Ireland, it would be madness to venture into, no matter how long I had been living in Ireland. Ulick always reminds me of a remark made by one of his colleagues: 'When two French writers meet a third, they always form an academy or found a literary magazine; when two Irish writers are joined by a third, a civil war breaks out!'

As strange as it may seem, there was never a civil war between us. We even managed to work together without any mood swings on his part. When it comes to his own work, Ulick is truly humble. Together, on several afternoons in a row in Tynagh, we reread the proofs of his diary, *A Cavalier Irishman (1970-1981)*, an exceptional record of a troubled time and of the world he inhabited in New York, London and Dublin. In those pages you can see his short phrases, his razor-sharp gaze, his sarcastic views on the pretensions of his contemporaries or, on the other hand, his sympathy for those torn apart by Irish society. The book, which like Evelyn Waugh's diaries (1911–1966) is untranslatable, is also a repertoire of Irish humour. He gets away with one night-time escapade by quoting a surgeon who is quizzed in a divorce case: 'Did you sleep with this woman?' 'I didn't shut my eyes once, Your Honour!'

Irish wit thrives on this type of ambiguity. I was surprised when Ulick asked me to help him with the proofs of his diaries. Most of the time what I read made me feel like an outsider. I didn't recognize three-quarters of the names quoted but they would probably not be familiar to most ordinary readers. It was a diary for the initiates, with its complicities and its weaknesses, the telegrammatic story of an apparently chaotic life; in truth, it was a life led with a ferocious discipline and a deep sense of his own mission, from which nothing could distract him. Was he right to ask me to be the final judge of a publication that would appeal to very few people? Or was he hoping that a distant view of recent events or ephemeral characters would act as a filter through the overly temporal side of his tale?

Other collaborations followed: a preface to his translations of Baudelaire's *Poems of the Damned*. Its publication was marked by a very enjoyable launch party at the French Institute in Dublin, presided over by Michael D. Higgins, who was briefly Minister for Culture, and, for longer, I hope, a Galway poet with a long mane of white hair. We were to read together, Ulick his translations, I the originals. I asked the young people who were not familiar with Baudelaire's work – if there were any – to leave the room before I read 'Léthé'. There was no movement towards the door. Higgins did an admirable imitation of poetic giddiness. During the small dinner party that followed (without the poet minister), Ulick mimicked his voice and its staccato delivery to perfection. Higgins' convoluted speech made me doubt his familiarity with Baudelaire.

Nor will I ever forget Ulick's excitement when, during the Dublin Theatre Festival, one of my plays, *Ariane*, was performed in an English adaptation by Fanny de Burgh Whyte. During the rehearsals he made it his own, directed the director and the actors, went up on stage, modified the costumes and the lighting, all for the good of the performance, I must say. His explosive personality vanished behind the man of the stage and the actor (he is also an actor – I hadn't mentioned that before). And not just any old actor either: whether on stage or on screen, notably in *An Offering of Swans*, he is a man of such grace and lyricism that he makes you forget all about the testy swordsman of Dublin literary gatherings. Not only did he give extremely intelligent analyses of the text to the actors, but from his seat he played all the roles with such piercing intelligence that all the young actors had to do was imitate him.

The theatre brought us together once more after that, curiously enough in Lot-et-Garonne, for a series of performances of his play *Execution* that my daughter Alice had just translated into French.

Execution deals with one of the most dramatic episodes in modern Irish history – a deadly confrontation between the freedom fighters in Ireland after the departure of the crown forces, and the establishment of a republican government. It wouldn't be accurate to say that it is an original piece of work. Ulick never hid the fact that he used the courtroom speeches for the prosecution and the defence, and the statements of the prison warders and the memoirs of the lawyers and witnesses in a respectful fashion, putting his great knowledge of the stage to good use. The result sent shivers down one's spine and aroused feelings of compassion that paralyzed the audience when we went to see the play in the Peacock Theatre in Dublin. No theatre in Paris was interested, but the Baladins acting troupe in Agen risked it, and it was worth it.

Ulick had come to see the show for himself and was staying in a country hotel in Lot-et-Garonne. In the morning, from my vantage in Monclar, I could see him leaving his hotel to join us, walking up the winding road that wends its way through the cornfields, advancing at a steady pace until he reached the village, with only his elegant panama hat to give him away.

He would sit inside the Baladin, the only café-bistro in the village, run by Huguette Pommier, an admirable woman whose intelligence and authority meant that, for a time, her village became an unforgettable centre of attraction. He had scarcely taken his seat before he began to complain that the actors had not already begun rehearsals in the tiny room next door. Despite people's extremely polite efforts to explain to him, he could not understand that the thirteen actors of *Execution* were also rehearsing a dozen other plays sometimes all night in secret – and that, from time to time, it was difficult for them to get up before midday.

Sitting near the door with a cup of coffee and a glass of water, wearing his blazer (even in its distressed state, you could still see that it was a blazer) and one of his fantastical ties, with his panama hat on the table next to him, Ulick would see the regulars coming in one by one. It has to be said that in Monclar there is a rest home, one of the last traces of the greedy profit of the III Republic that you don't often see anymore, a refuge for its lonely occupants who were not always that steady on their feet. During the day they are allowed out – at least those who don't get lost on the only street in the village – and, since there are no special attractions apart from the wonderful scenery surrounding the village's rocky peak, they hang out in (or hang onto) the bar for their first drink of the day. For the first hour, Ulick remained alone in their midst, obviously incapable of understanding what was being mumbled around him. Convinced that what was being said was friendly, he replied with a couple of words in English and they nodded in response; he smiled when they extended a greasy paw to him and declined when they offered him a glass of dry white wine or a drop of something stronger in his coffee. For a long time I wondered what the Baladin's regulars thought of him. In actual fact, with the exception of two or three of them, they probably didn't think anything of him at all, and an alien, like those portrayed in comic books with peduncular heads, six-fingered hands and mechanical voices, would have seemed less strange to them than this poet who had strayed into their village for reasons they could not make out, in spite of the publicity surrounding Theatre Night.

When *A Cavalier Irishman* was published (in London before it came out in Dublin), Ulick was interviewed for *The Irish Times* by Vincent Browne. Browne and Ulick had detested each other for thirty years; their relationship was punctuated by punches and – in a typical Ulickean drama – Ulick even accused Browne of having broken a pane of glass in his front door, while Browne accused Ulick of insulting the wife of a judge friend of his, in public, in a restaurant. The interview was a well-mannered affair, despite the fundamental discord that reigned between the two men, though Browne did admit to coming to Fairfield Park with the intention of starting the conversation with this charming opening line: 'How is it that civilized people invite you to lunch and dinner so often, given that you're such an unbearable and tireless braggart?'

What would have happened had he started with that thunderous declaration? Sometimes the gods smile on us. Ulick was in exceptionally good form. From the outset, he disarmed his interviewer. His book had already been well received by the British and American press. If the Irish critics didn't follow suit, it didn't matter; time would be the final judge. On 8th September 2001, there was a big photograph of Ulick in *The Irish Times*. I kept the page. Ulick is seated at his worktable, with his back turned to a glass-fronted case full of bound books, watched over by a bronze bust mounted on a stand. He is wearing a dressing-gown and looking at the photographer with a smile that is both benevolent and amused. The neck of his shirt is open. He has his arms crossed and has one elbow on the table. Near the right elbow, with a magnifying glass, one can see the title of a book that still has its dust jacket on – *Ulster 1969* – but our attention is drawn to another book that he holds in his inclined right hand, more of a brochure than a book really, with a very visible title, *Orangeism*. In the photo, which is not posed in a terribly naturalistic fashion, both titles remind the reader that the man who is interviewed here is constantly ready to defend the memory of a revolution that even if, like the catoblepas, it is consuming itself. Better yet, the spine of the thin book is facing the photographer and is, or seems to be, on fire, with a flame apparently lit by the pressure of Ulick's fingers running up it. When I asked him about it over the phone, Ulick's response was categorical.

'I have never burned a book and never will.'

Since I insisted, he concluded, 'I'll have to look at the photo again.'

I'm still waiting for his answer, but I would not have been surprised had the book caught fire in Ulick's hands after a particularly explosive conversation between *The Irish Times*'s interviewer and his volatile self.

8.

EVEN WHEN they are deprived of their basic rights, dispossessed of their lands, and their houses reduced to a heap of stones and smouldering thatch by the constables in the service of the occupants, people still have the freedom of speech to defy their oppressor and, if they are muzzled, they always have the one universal remedy for distress: they can use their inner voice to keep being themselves, or to be anyone else they choose – the darling heroes of their memory, the rich and the poor, the victors and the vanquished, the happy or deserted lover.

One by one, these wanderers who spill their interior monologues on the sides of the main roads, will undoubtedly disappear. On these free spirits a caring society places its constraints, encloses the last rebels in their charitable institutions, but I can never forget big Sarah, whom I met on my first journey. She wore a wide black skirt and waistcoat with huge boots and a multi-coloured shawl thrown over her shoulders, and had a long grey plait that hung down onto her chest. For centuries, she had been walking the roads of Donegal, Mayo and Connemara, miming an imaginary conversation with the dead with expressive gestures, swinging the bundle she was carrying filled with a few rags, cans of beer, and potatoes cooked in ashes, her only food.

There were scheduled stops in her journey that she was incapable of explaining both times I met her, but which, through a sort of animal instinct, she never varied – her journey was a closed circuit punctuated with obligatory halts, begun the day when the last of her six children died. In the villages, she rested in the grocers-cum-haberdashers-cum-post-office among the crazy bric-a-brac that disappeared each year to make way for faceless shops. People were kind-hearted there. They pulled up a chair for her, she sat down, tired and worn-out, leaned against the back of the chair and stretched out her long legs. The skirt, with all its pockets, was pulled up high enough to reveal a pair of purple, scabby calves over her shoes. I can still see her face – the nose of a Greek statue stuck in the noble visage of an Inca mummy, the forehead, the cheeks furrowed with wrinkles converging on lips which were still beautiful, despite her lack of teeth. Her provision of cans and potatoes were discretely renewed while she continued to talk uninterrupted, continuing the speech she started the day she left her house to walk, simply to walk and to talk to herself out loud, asking questions and providing the answers for the invisible interlocutors without varying the tone.

'I said:

'Stay!'

She said:

'No, I'm going with him.'

I said:

'He'll make you unhappy.'

She said:

'Me, unhappy with him?'

I said 'yes, with him, you'll be unhappy!'

She said:

'Mother, I will have my own children.'

Her brother said:

'He won't give you any children, he doesn't know how to f...'

I said:

'What do you know? You're not his wife.'

She said:

'My mother, I'm leaving.'

I said:

'He drinks.'

She said:

'I'll stop him.'

I said:

'Are you going to stop the world from turning too? And what about me? You are both saying filthy things. Your father, who is in Heaven with the Father, can hear you and he's waiting for you.'

She said:

'Tim was the one who said f..."

BY THE END of the afternoon she would be on the road again heading towards Maam Bridge at Leenane, standing tall and proud in the rain, walking in a way that's unusual in women – stubborn and steady with big strides, like a foot soldier. With one hand, she kept the swaying bundle in place over her shoulder. Her shawl was pulled up over her head and fastened under her chin by a big pin with a few strands of grey hair visible in front; hers was really a wild beauty, the reigning spirit of bogs, of dark water and of mountains lost in fog.

I pulled up when I drew level with her and rolled down the window. Her face was radiant with goodness, generosity and dreams. No, she didn't want a lift; she had time for herself – time that God gives us in such large quantities. There was cowardly relief on my part. How would I have got rid of the wild animal smell that would have lingered in the car long after she'd got out? And immediately afterwards, with me ignobly sitting inside, sheltered and hastily putting my window back up to keep out the cold and the damp, she stood in the icy drizzle and took up her monologue again.

'But I did tell them:

'Don't go, the sea is rough.'

He said:

'Mother, it's for the fish.'

I said:

'The fish will be there all the other days.'

He said:

'You never eat any.'

I said:

'Your life is worth more than a herring.'

He said:

'I'm not sure; that's the way it is anyway. I have three children. Who will feed them if I don't go out?'

I said:

'The Good Lord.'

He said:

'Then we'll be waiting a while; I'm going.'

I said:

'Farewell my beloved boy.'"

HUGE TEARS coursed down her cheeks. She stuck the bundle back on her shoulder and set off again down the road. Through the steamed-up windscreen I saw her stride away with her magnificent step that would take her all over the world… Well, all over her world – a patch of black earth scattered with bronze lakes, roads edged with fuchsia and rhododendron under which her six children and an invisible man slept. She was the last queen of the age of the Gaels, alas deprived of her golden shield, her leather helmet, her lance and her sword. One day she must have gone to sleep by the side of Lough Mask and sunk slowly into the springy earth where bull irises grow, spirits of the bog who delight in welcoming bodies exhausted by grief and immortal souls.

THEY ARE NOT all that wild. I have good memories of a fellow I gave a lift to one morning on the way out of Athlone: bareheaded, his face reddened more by beer than by the cold, squeezed into a black overcoat fastened with safety-pins.

'I can take you as far as Loughrea.'

'Loughrea will do me nicely. I'll get another breakfast in the shelter. I've already had one but two is better, and at Loughrea you can stay the night and head off the next day on a full stomach. I notice you have a German accent.'

'No, French.'

'It's the same as the German one.'

'I don't think so. Do you have friends in Loughrea?'

The idea sent him into gales of laughter.

'What's funny about that?'

'I'm a sailor. I don't have any friends.'

'So what are you doing?'

'I'm walking.'

'How long do you plan to do that?'

He shrugged after each question I asked but it resembled a tic rather than an attempt to quell my curiosity.

'What do I know? A year, maybe two. Or more. I just feel like walking. When I stop in Cork or in Dublin, I'll find a ship no trouble. I've already been to China, Africa ...'

I know this litany; it's always the same. Often they haven't set foot on dry land, or else if they've gone on a spree and got so drunk that they can't remember anything past the names of the places they stopped at. In any case, a sailor on foot is a rare occurrence, almost as rare as a sailor on horseback. The

84

car was heated. Unfamiliar with it and ill at ease, he started to wipe his forehead and to try and open his coat, but the rusty pins popped one after the other.

'Do you wear it when you sleep?'

He laughed again and asked for a cigarette.

'In the shelters there's only one blanket per bed. And last night I was a bit tight. Do you walk yourself?'

'Yes, yes I do, but for long journeys I prefer the car. What do you do while you're walking?'

'I think. I think about the choices in life. You think better when you walk.'

I wasn't going to talk to him about the great walkers from Goethe to Eckermann. A little before Ballinasloe, a small car came hurtling down the middle of the road. I had to pull in to the left and nearly ended up with two wheels in the ditch. In the brand new vehicle, there were four nuns. The one who was driving was hunched over the wheel.

I said, 'The nuns are driving fast this year.'

'Irish nuns are the fastest in the world. Wait and see what they'll be like next year when they have their driving licence.'

We could have had even more fun if, when driving through Ballinasloe, he hadn't run his tongue over his lips several times.

'There's a nice little pub here – Joe's place. It's so hot in your car. Enough to make you die of thirst.'

'Pints of stout at eleven o'clock in the morning? No thanks. And at no other time for that matter.'

'The problem if I drink by myself is that I'm broke.'

No one could remain hard-hearted faced with such an admission. I put two pounds, sorry punts, into his hand.

'That's not what I meant.'

'I would have given them to you anyway, even if you hadn't asked for them.'

'Well, I'm a right fool!'

He got out of the car, he turned up the collar of his coat and strode towards Joe Goran's pub. Before pushing open the door, he stopped and saluted me with a two-fingered victory sign.

I never saw him again, but whenever I hear a recording of the ballad 'Come Ye Tramps and Hawkers' by The Dubliners, I think of him.

> *Oftentimes I've laughed untae mysel when trudgin' on the*
> *road*
> *My toerags round my blistered feet, my face as broon's a toad*
> *…*
> *An' if the weather treats me right I'm happy every day.*

In K, right next to us, live the Barnetts. Rumour has it, they come from somewhere else; that is to say, the road. One day a boy left the family caravan pulled by a piebald pony and went to work in a farm, far away from his own people. He worked hard, bought a horse that was only skin and bone, looked after it and sold it on for three times the price. He was their great-grandfather, and he lived at the start of the twentieth century. His tricks gave him the means to buy patches of ground here and there, to marry a settled woman, and to have a child: unfortunately only one, Ciaron.

I knew Ciaron, and he had seven children and perhaps thirty grandchildren. They grew and expanded, built houses, bought woodland and meadows and then Ciaron, now a patriarch, had a heart attack. Because he was Herculean in stature, he pulled through with a lame leg and a shaking hand that he kept in his pocket, but in the meantime his eldest took things in hand – the horses, the cows and the sheep. Ciaron watched him in silence. Every hour he had to be given a cup of tea. He recovered the power of speech and grew thin. His sly eyes traced all the comings and goings of his wife and son. The old travelling gene awoke in his blood and he started to get itchy feet – one was working fine, the other followed willy-nilly. Mrs Barnett knew it and locked the doors, keeping the keys in her apron pocket. But he wasn't a man who could be locked up easily. Despite his handicap, he took advantage of every second when his wife's head was turned, or the grandchildren's, as they came in and out non-stop. They'd pick him up on the road and he'd come home in high spirits as if he'd played a clever trick on them. Unaware of all this, I came across him one morning as I was driving out of the village, and he waved his stick at me.

'Where are you headed, sir?'

'Galway.'

'That's great, I'm going there too.'

He was one of the old school, and still said 'sir'. He even used other formalities that had long disappeared from the countryside. I dropped him off at Eyre Square and offered to collect him in an hour to bring him back to K. There was no need: he was meeting some friends, they would take him home. That very evening the matriarch phoned me.

'I know you took him to Galway.'

'He was going there.'

'Ciaron is a born liar.'

Three days later he hitched a lift home, grinning from ear to ear, delighted with his adventure, unchanged except that he had lost his gabardine somewhere en route, but wearing his flat cap and rubber boots (wellingtons they call them here) as usual. He'd bought a calf and a horse along the way, leaving what could be deemed a down payment of honour, fifty pence, for each of them. The rest of the sum was to be completed when his eldest son went to collect them with his cattle truck. Where had he eaten, drunk, slept, washed himself along the way? No one knows. Mrs Barnett doesn't speak to me anymore – so at least the tale had a silver lining.

IN KILLINADEEMA, a long road climbs over the hill; at the top there is an admirable view of Lough Rea and the plain. The roadway is so narrow, you can only move at twenty miles an hour, and I let the dogs out before reaching the forest to get them warmed up. They love that and bound along like mad things. When you come across another car – a rare occurrence – you have to reverse or park in a gateway. On the hill, a picturesque cemetery overlooks the lake and the fields, none of which are ever the same shade of green. Every time I go there, I come across a tall, thin, ramrod straight man wearing a round tweed hat and a large canary-yellow oilskin coat. He walks at a brisk clip from morning to evening with his hands in his pockets, going and back and forth along the road from Gort to Aille Cross. When the dogs pass him and the car draws near, he raises his left hand and points his index finger at the sky, without turning round. In Naples this would be an insult. Here it is a friendly sign. One day a serious study of national signs used by the companionship of walkers should be undertaken, since they are never the same and often contradictory. If we see each other, he raises a finger to his hat and I flick on my indicator in reply. After questioning him a little, I discovered his name was Liam. He is retired and has come from Galway to live with his daughter, who is a nurse at the regional hospital.

One morning the dogs had disappeared in pursuit of a hare and I stopped to wait for them. Liam drew level with me and asked, 'What age are you?'

At once he'd bypassed the usual phrases that start ordinary conversations, those eternal conversations about the rain, the wind or the good weather, each equally detestable, and which annoy me very quickly. I admitted my age.

'I'm nine years older than you and I'm in good health. Believe me, all those tablets are rubbish. A two-hour walk, morning and afternoon, and you'll live to be a hundred.'

In his smooth face, with its marble skin, his blue eyes were veiled by the beginning of cataracts. His mouth had no lips and big dark hairs protruded from his nostrils and ears.

'Health,' he said, 'is better than wealth. It really is, you know. In 1938 I went to Dublin for the first time to see a football match. Dublin was playing Galway. When I got off the train I asked for directions. The employee, a fat one-armed man with a red poppy in his buttonhole, looked at me as if I were a foreigner. When he recovered from his surprise, he said, "Follow the crowd, it's going straight to Lansdowne Road. Can't go wrong." I saw the match and Galway won.'

He bent down, picked up a few pebbles and used them to show me how Galway made the winning kick. The demonstration was not very clear and I had to pretend to be following it with interest, even though I didn't know if he was talking about soccer or Gaelic football, a mixture of rugby and soccer. With the outside of his foot, he pushed away the pebbles.

'No one plays like that anymore. Young people have too much money. They go to the pub, watch videos; they all have cars and motorbikes. They don't walk anymore. The most important thing is your health. Wealth doesn't count.'

He raised a finger to his cap and set off again. A moment later the dogs came back, and I passed him on the road. Without deigning a backward glance, he gave me a little Neapolitan sign.

THE WEATHER was good, but it wasn't necessarily summer; it might have been winter or one of those intermediate seasons. The main thing, anyway, was that the weather was nice. We had lunched on the lawn in front of the house, and I had stayed there by myself to read next to my cold coffee, with one of the dogs snoring under the shade of the parasol. It is always difficult to read in the open air – a bird whizzed by in the sky, bees were buzzing in the fuchsia bushes. I forget what I was reading. It can't have been very interesting. My eyes would often wander from the page, or else I felt like getting up at the slightest thing that popped into my head, convinced that if I didn't do it right away, I'd forget all about it.

He was walking down the fuchsia-lined drive, between the two flamboyant hedges that trembled in the least puff of wind. So it must have been summer, probably even August – fuchsias come into bloom quite late. I didn't recognize the head that I could see over the hedges, nor the whole man when I saw him emerging at the end of the lane and crossing the lawn in my direction. He was a frail man of about forty at most, in a blue striped suit with bellbottom trousers, a white shirt and a fluorescent tie that looked particularly out of place in the middle of the country, with the sun shining down on us. The strangest thing of all was his head: he had a yellowish face and a mass of tight blue-black corkscrew ringlets for hair – really very curly and parted in the centre. He would have made you laugh if he hadn't such a dark, questioning look, with an intensity that reminded me of Dr Roumerguère, a psychoanalyst who once came to talk to me about Dali and whom I had the greatest difficulty in getting rid of without calling out the fire-brigade. But this visitor looked rather shy and if his decision to visit had been, no doubt, well thought out, finding himself in front of me must have troubled him to the extent that he remained silent with his arms by his sides, biting his lips, comically displaced at the bottom of a garden on a sunny afternoon, wearing a city suit that no one else would be seen in for miles around except maybe the solicitor, while I sat there in my shirt sleeves with a book on my knees. In the end I said, 'I imagine you want to see my wife. She's the one who looks after the horses; I know nothing about them. She won't be back before six o'clock.'

A charming, almost childlike smile illuminated his face, erasing the nervousness I had suspected, or if it wasn't nervousness, more likely the astonishment of being there had just abruptly woken him up from a dream.

It was as if I had suddenly turned the key in a mechanical toy: he joined his hands in humble prayer and an imploring expression lit up his sad face.

'Oh no! I haven't come to talk about horses; I'm a poet. I'm going to write poems and since you are a very well-known writer I would like you to help me to get them published. It's of great importance.'

Now things were getting interesting. He sat down on the edge of a garden chair. His knobbly knees stuck out through his well-ironed trousers, and despite the care taken over them, he wore no wedding ring on his left hand. You could picture him as the best man, a white carnation in his buttonhole, sitting against the wall while the more daring guests invited the bride's friends to dance. He listened to me seriously, although not really convinced by my down-to-earth arguments – publishers are in no rush to publish poetry collections, I was a French writer and published mostly in France, and even if I had the least influence with an English publisher, it seemed necessary to me that he should write his poems first ...

Of course … He did have some rough drafts but nothing that he could show me and what he really wanted, before he got down to it, was the certainty that he would be published. He was very disappointed that I could give him no such guarantees, there on the lawn in front of the house on a nice summer afternoon the like of which we rarely see; he accused the publishers of being interested only in profit, never in art. In the end, I was able to ask him what he read. Yeats, he said. He hadn't had the time to read many other writers yet.

The conversation was dragging on and when, to liven things up, he told me that it was fine and hot, and that neither rain nor wind was expected for the evening, I admitted that I wanted to work and said that I hoped to see him again when he was satisfied with his poetic output. To get rid of him, I suggested that I would walk with him as far as the gate where he had left his car, bike or motorcycle.

'I go everywhere on foot,' he said, 'I live near Abbey. It's not far from here, not far from anything at all.'

Six miles from Tynagh, where we were at that very minute, six to Portumna, twelve to Loughrea. Each afternoon he went to one of those places and walked back at the end of the day. I asked if we could calculate all the journeys back and forth at the same time for three hundred and sixty-five days per year.

'In five years, at that speed, you would have walked round the world.'

'It would be interesting; I'd love to see new places, but in the meantime everything would be covered with dust.'

He had a favourite pub in both towns, and from time to time he would have a drink in our village. He wasn't a big drinker. When he had too much, he couldn't think about his poems. The whole journey was for one pint, after which he went home. An indiscreet question was nagging away at me – what do you live off when you do nothing?

'I left the farm to my brother. He gave me a cottage so I could write my poems. He's a very good man. I hope he will never marry. I probably wouldn't get on with his wife. I know women – they always want you to talk to them.'

Had he never thought of buying a bicycle?

'Certainly not. That would be the end of my inspiration. I'd have to press on the pedals, and pay attention to the cars, but on foot everything is automatic, you don't have to worry about anything. Your head does all the work. If I calculate correctly my poems will run to several volumes, maybe three or four. Perhaps I'm exaggerating because often I can't remember the beautiful things that have gone through my head. Poetry is like dreams. In any case, I'm very pleased to have met you. We'll do good work together whenever you want.'

Since then I've seen him once or twice on the road, going back and forth to his pub. Over time his fiercely curly hair has started to turn grey but he is still as elegant as ever, in his own way, with his city suit in the countryside, always deep in thought. There is no point in hoping for a Neopolitan sign from him. Almost fifteen years elapsed before we met again, in Portumna on the footpath across the road from the post office; he was wearing a camel-hair (or imitation camel hair) coat and was carrying an umbrella. The only thing missing was a bowler hat. I was dressed like a country bumpkin in my oilskin, flat hat and boots.

'How are your poems going? I'm looking forward to reading them.'

'Oh, they're coming on, coming on ... I've been putting together bits and pieces. Your publisher has to be patient.'

9.

ON THE WAY from Loughrea to Gort, the turn off for Thoor Ballylee was so badly signposted that I missed it twice, despite the fact that I had often gone there alone or with friends afflicted by Yeatsomania. The narrow road snaked in and out between the fields, fenced off by rows of Cyclops-like stones, before heading down into a trench of hedges. The tower appeared by surprise in the middle of a clearing of elms and oaks. At its foot, a bridge fords a lazy river of copper-coloured water – farther ahead, the Cloon disappears from view into the ground.

With its stone-cut walls adorned with no other asperity than a gargoyle roughly sculpted from a jutting stone, Thoor Ballylee resembles a prison. Its few windows are blocked with iron bars.

Swallows fly in and out of the spy holes. From the outside, it radiates suicidal austerity. What on earth gave Yeats the notion of setting up home in that icy, almost sightless tomb? He who in his youth claimed to be 'Pre-Raphaelite in every way'?

The tower would not be worth the trip had Yeats not ennobled it and protected it from the advancing decay that threatens the last remaining markers of a fierce foreign occupation. Did he really live there? Not that often, if my sources are to be believed ... Well, from time to time, long enough for his name to be linked with it forever. He often preferred the hospitality of Lady Gregory at Coole Park, a couple of miles from Thoor Ballylee:

> *I, the poet William Yeats,*
> *With old mill boards and sea-green slates,*
> *And smithy work from the Gort forge,*
> *Restored this tower for my wife George;*
> *And may these characters remain*
> *When all is ruin once again.*

Because of the frenetic advance of cultural tourism, the entrance to the tower is now via a thatched cottage where all the inevitable horrors are arrayed – things like green scarves, green caps, green shields adorned with shamrocks. That day, two 'ladies' in severe black suits (not green, they must be sick of it) were selling tickets. Even though I was the morning's only visitor, I didn't seem to bother them too much. The younger of the two guided me to a large empty room where rows of benches were facing a screen; she switched off the light and turned on the projector. What appeared on the screen wasn't a film, but a series of extremely well mounted sepia photographs showing Yeats' childhood, youth, middle age, the friends who accompanied him in his literary life and contributed to the Celtic Renaissance, the women of his heart and his intellect: Lady Gregory, who was the spitting image of Queen Victoria; Maud, 'a being from another world', and Iseult Gonne, mother and daughter more beautiful than fairies; Countess Markievicz as a dreamy young girl and later as a revolutionary with a pistol; his wife Georgie Hyde-Lees who looks quite intimidating and like she was already in touch with the spirit world; and finally William Butler Yeats, in a completely perfect half-length portrait, wearing an open beige coat over a white shirt that is a bit slack for his powerful neck, a light-coloured felt hat with the brim turned up, as was the fashion with artists in the twenties, and no drooping pussy-bow, but a bright bow tie. He is not smiling, but you can tell he's pleased to have been snapped at that precise moment of the day – his fleshy mouth cuts the lower part of his face; his eyes are slightly slanted behind a pince-nez, from which a black cord, tied to the collar of the shirt, dangles for reassurance; his straight nose leads to a very sensual upper lip. In a diary entry from 1930 he writes, 'always particular about my clothes, never dissipated, never unshaven ...' but he discovered a completely different side to himself in the portrait of him made by the painter Augustus John: 'I saw myself there an unshaven, drunken bar-tender, and then I began to feel John had found something that he liked in me, something closer than character, and by that very transformation made it visible. He had found Anglo-Irish solitude, a solitude I have made for myself, an outlawed solitude.' What would he have thought of the admirable posthumous portraits painted of him by Louis le Brocquy: death masks on the point of liquefaction, a terrible silence ...

I kept the images of this brief reminder of a life in mind during the rest of my visit, with an anthology in hand:

> *A winding stair, a chamber arched with stone,*
> *A grey stone fireplace with an open hearth,*
> *A candle and written page.*
> Il Penseroso*'s* Platonist *toiled on*
> *In some like chamber, shadowing forth*
> *How the daemonic rage*
> *Imagined everything.*
> *Benighted travellers*
> *From markets and from fairs*
> *Have seen his midnight candle glimmering.*

A room with a wooden ceiling painted blue and yellow occupied the first floor. In an alcove, protected by a glass front, there was a wicker chair that looked like it would fall to pieces at any moment. The curator of Thoor Ballylee was no fetishist – he could not confirm that the poet liked the seat. In another glass case were some of Yeats' first editions, all of them dusty or covered with damp stains. The trestles and planks that Yeats evokes in his 'Meditations in Time of Civil War' have disappeared. For the benefit of visitors whose imagination confines writers to sitting behind their desks, a table of varnished wood had replaced Yeats' actual improvised set-up. Unfortunately, the table looked very small for such a great œuvre, that hoped to unite and reconcile Protestant and Catholic myths at the heart of national, and later European, literature.

The room, barely lit by the sparse daylight, was icy cold. The thickness of the walls isolated it from all sounds of the world outside. Temptation stops at the door of Thoor Ballylee, where Yeats' work mastered the fervent enthusiasm of youth and also its first sorrows. There, he blossomed as a writer, having distanced himself from inflammatory politics; the message of the poet went beyond national quarrels and frontiers. At Thoor Ballylee, Yeats came into his own. He had twenty more years in front of him to free himself of the chains shackling his universality, and four years to see his thought crowned with the Nobel Prize: 'I see the ghosts of hate and a heart too full, and a void announced …'

You can imagine him, such a tall man, walking with measured steps in those lugubrious rooms, bending his head under the very low lintels of the doorways or turning sideways to climb the stairs, too narrow for a man of his build. On the floor above, under the open roof terrace, lay his bedroom: 'Up high in the tower, I lean on the broken stone. Like powdery snow, fog trails over everything …'

It is easy to understand why Yeats frequently strayed just out of Coole Park for a breath of fresh air at the home of the muse of the Celtic Revival, Lady Gregory. It had a religiously literary atmosphere, and brought him comfort after his life as a hermit. Coole House is more like a manor house than a chateau. There, he was surrounded by respect and fervour. Unfortunately, those were the final glory days of an extraordinary woman. Lady Gregory was married to the cause of Irish liberty, with great freedom of spirit and tenacity. This was made all the more remarkable because in her manner and discourse she was a caricature of the landowning Anglo-Irish class who, since the time of Cromwell, had pillaged and subjugated Ireland. But, as is often the case, masters and servants resemble each other. For Lady Gregory, the world was divided into those who owned a toothbrush and the foot soldiers who did not. At the same time, she defended Sean O'Casey's first play, *The Shadow of a Gunman*, and invited him into her home – he was a communist who scandalized the servants by arriving without a tie or even a collar on his shirt. Even though she had allowed herself the right to do so since her marriage to Sir William Gregory (who died in 1892), she made a rule of not discussing politics with other women. Of Miss Horniman, an Englishwoman from Manchester, rich heiress to a tea magnate's fortune and most of all patron of the Abbey Theatre founded by Yeats and Lady Gregory herself, she said with the kind of aristocratic disdain you'd expect: 'I think it an error to treat merchants as if they had the same values as us.'

She hated the wives of her writer friends. Her name, or rather that of her husband Sir William, is linked with an eviction law, the infamous Gregory Clause dating from the Great

Famine of 1845–1852, when he had the British parliament ensure that any tenant farmer who hadn't paid his rent arrears would be evicted from his farm by the police and his house razed to the ground. Of course none of this was Lady Gregory's fault, but in her attitude she retained the whiff of pitiless aristocratic disdain for the poverty of that awful time. She never said 'a catholic', she said 'a papist', even at the time when she set up a Gaelic school in Kiltartan, her parish. Yeats was summoned to honour the school and composed a poem from which, out of charity, I only quote two lines:

> *My country is Kiltartan Cross,*
> *My countrymen Kiltartan's poor.*

The school, which has been converted into a museum, is a masterpiece of bad taste, even by Irish standards where the competition is fierce. It could be taken for a train station in a coal-mining outpost. The charming lady who sells tickets at the desk – no tacky souvenirs there – will look like Lady Gregory in a couple of years. With the exception of three important letters, the exhibition is of no interest: newspaper cuttings, photos, posters, a few books and, in the back room, a recreated classroom. It's got everything: inkwells, exercise books, pens, a blackboard, desks, and, at the front of the room, in a long skirt, a mannequin of a pretty school teacher that looks as if it might fly off like Mary Poppins. Nothing really inspiring. For the sake of good manners, when I'd finished looking round the 'museum' I stopped at the charming lady's desk, and she asked me for the two-euro entry fee.

In a nonchalant fashion, she reorganized the few brochures and postcards that were scattered in the display case, hoping to tempt me. Behind me, an old couple in matching red parkas and oversized bushwhacker hats were getting impatient. I was still foraging in my pocket to find the right change, when the old man joyfully explained: 'We've just arrived from Australia this morning. From Canberra. My name is Murphy, Seamus Murphy. My sister is Moira, Moira Murphy ... Our family come from Gort. We're paying our first visit to the land of our ancestors.'

'Granddad was in the service of Lady Gregory.'

'Granddad often spoke of Lady Gregory.'

'We're very excited. It's a joy for us to finally come and visit Coole House.'

'Granddad said it was the most beautiful house in the west.'

Behind the counter the lady was truly sorry. In the same cautious tone used to announce a recent death to a family member, she said she was obliged to tell them that, although Kiltartan's school was restored and housed keepsakes of Lady Gregory, Coole House itself was demolished in 1947. Its new owner, the Irish State, sold it to a wrecker. The materials, stone, woodwork, fireplaces, were used to build a dozen identical bungalows that run alongside Gort.

'You're joking!' the little man exclaimed in a trembling voice. 'Someone would have told us. Granddad was in Lady Gregory's service for ten years. We've come from Australia ...'

'From Canberra!' his sister added, as if that made things even more unimaginable.

'I don't come from as far away, just from Tynagh,' I said, 'and I heard about the demolition of Coole House a year ago. Luckily, Coole Park hasn't been turned into a developers' lot. You should go and visit it.'

'It's very well looked after,' said the lady at the counter. 'And it's only ten minutes away.'

A bus had dropped them off and the next one was not due until midday, so I offered to give them a lift as I was going to Coole Park myself. The dog waiting in the car intrigued them.

'It looks like a Labrador. Granddad had one of them.'

'No, it's a Weimaraner, a German breed.'

'Ah, so you're German!'

'Absolutely not. The owners of Pekinese are not necessarily all Chinese.'

I felt that they wanted to know more, so I said, 'I'm French.'

'Granddad,' said Seamus, 'went to France in 1914; he was a volunteer in a regiment of Irish Fusiliers. He was decorated.'

'A volunteer!' Moira echoed. 'We have the medal and the certificate to prove it.'

Despite their Australian accents, which are not always easy to decipher, I understood that they were born in 1940, and that these two 'old people' were in fact twenty years younger than me.

The gate to Coole Park was wide open; a sign indicated that it would close at 9pm, a precaution useful for discouraging joy-riders, who play stock-car racing with stolen cars and abandon the burnt-out wrecks in its most beautiful forests. We left the car in the car park and walked to the site where

Coole House once stood. The space was left empty – just a lawn, surrounded by grey walls.

'It's a good job that Granddad is no longer with us,' sighed Seamus. 'He'd have a heart-attack.'

They wanted to accompany me on my walk, but I'd had more than enough of Granddad.

'The trails are signposted. There's no danger of getting lost. And to be honest, I like walking by myself to talk to myself in my head.'

'You talk to yourself in your head?' asks Moira in a worried tone.

'Yes, I meditate.'

'Granddad liked meditating too. He would walk for hours in the mountains with his dog.'

'You won't get lost. There are signposts everywhere. Good luck.'

They were pathetic, I grant you, but I couldn't take on all the pathetic cases in the world and the memories of their granddads. A hundred metres away, they would find a visitors' centre, a map of the forest, and postcards. Farewell, dear Murphys, I like to walk alone in the steps of the poet. The path ran alongside a meadow; a group of children were playing there under the supervision of a monitor.

When Yeats escaped from sinister Thoor Ballylee to take the air at Coole House, he switched centuries. In her old age – Lady Gregory was sixty-seven in 1919 – she took great pains to maintain the grand ceremony of the pre-war period. She still kept servants; the house was heated. If the wine cellar was empty – Yeats was largely responsible for this – the food was still good. The future Nobel Prize winner (1923) began to go there as a paying guest, which offset his place at table for Lady Gregory. She wasn't even an usufructuary anymore; her son was killed in the war and the property now belonged to her daughter-in-law; she preferred to live in Galway, probably to avoid the hassle. Appearances were kept up, Lady Gregory remained mistress of the house and her admiration for Yeats endured, despite the fact that he claimed authorship of *Cathleen Ni Houlihan*, a play she wrote and to which he made a few minor corrections. A preface and a poem he wrote about the death of her son, Robert Gregory, offended her. She forgot about them, or pretended to forget. The cause they had both been serving for so long was more important than all that pettiness. He was the guest of honour every time he visited. It is easy to get used to a throne. Yeats never got down from his.

In front of a bench where Lady Gregory was often photographed stands a magnificent copper beech, whose trunk is railed off to protect the signatures, or simply initials, cut into the bark: Bernard Shaw, the two Yeats brothers – the painter and the poet, Sean O'Casey, John Masefield, J.M. Synge, and other less well-known names, but all participants in the Celtic Renaissance. The shadow of the beech has burned the lawn. Yeats remembered the walk of the old lady in her kingdom:

> *Sound of a stick upon the floor, a sound*
> *From somebody that toils from chair to chair;*

The path wended its way under the vertiginous trees, pines and beeches. A milky light fell from the sky between the branches as they strained under the bounds of the squirrels:

> *Come play with me;*
> *Why should you run*
> *Through the shaking tree*
> *As though I'd a gun*
> *To strike you dead?*
> *When all I would do*
> *Is to scratch your head*
> *And let you go.*

Farther down, hidden by the foliage, a lake glimmered, surrounded by grasslands and edged by *f* reeds. From a belvedere, a wooden lectern displayed other verses by Yeats:

> *The trees are in their autumn beauty,*
> *The woodland paths are dry,*
> *Under the October twilight the water*
> *Mirrors a still sky;*
> *Upon the brimming water among the stones*
> *Are nine and fifty swans.*

That was an exaggeration. There were perhaps five or six swans gliding along, without making a ripple on the brimming waters of Coole Lough. The sky was bright; the silence was great. Not a soul to be seen. Apart from the swans, but do swans have souls? The sky was tragically empty, the silence so perfect as to drew you into it irresistibly, like an abyss.

I know that I shall meet my fate
Somewhere among the clouds above;

I came back along another path lined with trees whose trunks stretched so high that you would think they were sequoias. Returning from abroad, Anglo-Irish landowners brought essences from Asia or North America that then flourished in Ireland: aspens, maples, cedars, silver birches. It would have been nice to see some deer crossing the path. There were some, but no more than ten or so, flaming red in colour and lying in the high grass, cooped up in an enclosure, uninterested in the onlookers who lamented their fate. Yeats would return to Coole House by that same path, with dead leaves rustling underfoot:

Dim Pairc-na-carraig, where the wild bees fling
Their sudden fragrances on the green air;
Dim Pairc-na-tarav, where enchanted eyes
Have seen immortal, mild, proud shadows walk;
Dim Inchy wood, that hides badger and fox
And marten-cat, and borders that old wood
Wise Biddy Early called the wicked wood:
Seven odours, seven murmurs, seven woods.

A few days later, Alice accompanied me to Sligo (Sligeach!) As she was driving, I only had to look at the road. I hadn't been back to the north to Tuam, Claremorris or Charlestown, for years. I had loved the noble white houses with their black and white gables, the last thatched roofed cottages, the roads blocked with migrating cattle or runaway horses chewing the rich grass that grew on the verges. Encircled by a flock of sheep, we would stop in a sea of frizzy white wool, surrounded by an odour of sweat and the frightened bleating of lambs. We were never impatient, however – all in good time. Once we were freed from the sheep, a tall, thin, ageless fellow would usually appear wearing wellingtons and a flat cap stiff with mud glued to his head; he would bless us with his staff: 'Grand weather we're having!'

We'd stop the windscreen wipers and roll down the window. A burst of freezing air would catch us by the throat. Grand weather indeed; it could be worse.

But now, the cattle no longer migrate along trunk roads, and the weather seems less damp and windy. New roads cross the spruced-up countryside, which is no longer dotted with the hulks of cars and old tubs used previously as water-troughs, but that is fenced in more and more by barbed wire, strung between concrete posts.

What had become of the hedgerows of hawthorn, brambles and fuchsia? EU directives had also forced people to build barns and now, in winter, the landscape looks abandoned, lifeless and soulless. We no longer stop to allow a herd of jersey cows go by, but to allow the police to check car tax, insurance, or the colour of the diesel. The Minister for Tourism wants to put an end to Ireland's reputation as the 'Rip Off Republic'. Easier said than done!

The landscape in County Sligo is sometimes bucolic, and at others dramatically defiled by new buildings that spring up chaotically like poisonous mushrooms, adding new colours to the already rich Galway palette: sweetheart pink, goose-dropping yellow, almond green, butcher red, coffee cream, all pierced with the same standard windows and net-curtains. Jolly gnomes, stupid geese, swans and clay cats watch over prim and proper front gardens. Oh my dears, what are you doing to one of the most poetic countries in Europe?

Prosperity has come crashing down on Ireland like paedophilia on base clergymen. Would Yeats recognize his beloved Sligo? While the heart of the town has not changed, cars – the epidemic that afflicts old countries – have asphyxiated the narrow streets. Sometimes you can barely get around on foot. I am not sure that I recognize the aristocratic Sligo of the Sixties either in this joyous, variegated town, enlivened by the beautiful young people at large, sitting slumped on seats in the restaurants and pubs that line the canal. Everywhere you go, you are pursued by music being thumped out on loudspeakers.

The browse around the bookshops that I always begin my Sligo visits with was a bit of a disappointment. In a shed, a little leafy-shirted lady in tight jeans and heavy fake jewellery runs a swop shop where you bring in a book you have read and, in exchange for a modest subscription, leave with another, usually a yellowing old bestseller. A few years earlier at a Yeats conference in Ballina, Pierre Joannon and I had discovered one of those second-hand bookshops we both love, set up in the basement of an old house – the owner knew everything about Yeats and County Sligo. We went through heaps of books, stacked on the tiled floor or piled up chaotically on the shelves, until we were exhausted. It was a real bookworm's paradise. He spoke perfect French as well, might I add. Regrettably, the three bookshops in Sligo had since been renovated. In shops as attractive as supermarkets, the books were ordered by category. The Yeats section was the best stocked, with not just his complete works but also the by-products: essays, not all of them written in praise of the poet.

Frustrated at finding nothing interesting, we headed for Rosses Point, where our poet used to stay during the summer with his extended family. Of his childhood holidays he wrote: 'In fact, of my holidays I remember only my woes ... They were not caused by my family but by myself, I invented them.' As if it were for him that Terence, and much later Baudelaire, wrote 'L'Héautontimorouménos' ('Self Tormentor'), and he would continue to torment himself until his retirement and death in Roquebrune-Cap-Martin.

Just beyond Sligo, the inlet brought in the sea breeze. Between the road and the lagoon, hidden properties were huddled in vegetation as lush as that of Kerry. On the other side of the road were the usual bungalows, some closed restaurants and some deserted snack bars. At that time of day, the low sky was grey and we could hear the rapidly rising tide rushing through the channel. There are no words to describe that closed ground that would be overrun with water by the end of the afternoon – the grass was sparse, burnt by salt and iodine. Nonetheless, this was where John Butler Yeats, painter and father of the poet, read *The Lays of Ancient Rome* to his son William, dreary reading for a child who dreamed of a sailor's life. Everything was contradictory in Yeats' education before his days of glory. Nothing in the elegance of his being, the lyricism of his thought or his physical constitution pushed him towards a life as an adventurer, so he became a rebellious intellectual and a star-struck lover – the perfect recipe for a poet.

Dead horses used to be buried in the sludge on Rosses Point. The huge ocean dies there in the waves that break exhausted on the strand, or shatter on the cliffs. In the sky, a ballet of seagulls, herring gulls and, if I'm not mistaken, petrels play with the kites that are float above a creek of yellow sand. Fathers have great fun with toys they gave their children. For the Yeats family, tradition had it that a dream of a seabird foretold a death, or some great danger that threatened a family member. The birds are not wrong. The life of Erin is always in peril. If it wasn't for the deep thinkers keeping them alive, its history, its nightmares, its wondrous dreams and its extraordinary capacity to escape wearying reality and live on fantasies would be forgotten forever.

Rosses Point, and a few miles north, Drumcliff, draw their mystery and attraction from a majestic rocky table, which is marked with deep grooves cut into the grey stone by running water – I almost wrote 'tears'. Standing on the coast, like a challenge issued to the west, Benbulben is one of nature's enigmas. What forces and what furies raised this gigantic pebble festooned with a green skirt up out of the ground and cynically abandoned it there to intimidate the ocean? Benbulben is rooted like a monstrous meteorite washed up on Earth after a long voyage through space or after a burst of anger of subterranean spirits. Without the Titans and the Cyclops, mythology would never explain the chaos of the world. Since the beginning of time, myths have corresponded more clearly with existential questions than with incoherent reasoning. Men have never needed reason, but they do need the supernatural. As a child, Yeats never saw Benbulben without feeling frightened. Around him, his grandfather's servants and sailors and his young friends peopled Benbulben with monsters with dogs' heads and snakes' bodies, leprechauns with rattling laughter who promised great wealth to the people ready to give them change for a farthing, or the witch Vera whose magic wand transformed thieves and intruders into stone. These tales of witches aroused a feeling of repulsion for old women that stayed with Yeats throughout his life.

The most extravagant tales also had a humorous side: a shepherd had bet that he would throw himself into a cursed pond. He threw himself naked into the pond to disappear for ever, it seemed, but a few days later sent a message from Australia asking for his clothes to be forwarded to him. If you went astray on Benbulben or around Glencar Lough, you would meet the ghosts of loved ones, heroes and heroines who had been in the otherworld for a long time, good or evil spirits, seeking to wreak vengeance or offer guidance. Saint Columba came to pray there before he departed to found monasteries on the Continent and to save the sacred texts. Legend has it that when he was invited to dinner by a rich lady on Coney Island in Sligo Bay, instead of being served rabbit he was served a poor cat, roasted but apparently not dead, because when the animal was about to be cut up on the saint's plate it jumped up and came back to life. Benbulben acts on people's spirits like a crystal ball. When contemplating its broad silhouette, you can see the difficult and bloody stages of the birth of the Celtic nation – Ferdia confronting his friend Cú Chulainn from dawn to dusk to defend the rights of beautiful Queen Maeve. At nightfall, the two combatants dressed each others' wounds. Ferdia yielded to Cú Chulainn in the end and he, worshipped by women, was slain in turn by the valiant Conall, who had neither his aura not his worth. Beset by remorse, Conall dug Cú Chulainn's grave himself, and Némé, the hero's love, was buried alive alongside him.

Yeats dreamed throughout his life of the treasures of *Mirabilia Hibernia*, to the extent that in his final years he allowed himself wander in the clouds of astrology and esotericism; his wife, Georgie Hyde Lees, indulged in automatic writing.

If Yeats had the power to return to Benbulben, like the reincarnated ghosts of his childhood, his surprise (and probably his indignation) would be great when he saw the use the hotel industry has made of his family name for commercial purposes; it can be seen on Bed and Breakfasts, restaurants, and on every huckster's shop between Sligo and Drumcliff. What oversight is stopping County Sligo from being renamed County Yeats?

In a sort of inn, which of course bore the name of the poet, kind serving girls with bright eyes and cheeks rosy and glittering from the toing and froing between the kitchen and the dining-room ran between the tables and set down steaming plates of breaded plaice and a mountain of potatoes in front of us. The general odour of the dining-room was one of mingled cabbage and warm beer, which, on account of the smoking ban, could no longer be masked by the smell of tobacco. I looked around – had Irish people put on so much weight in the last few years, without me noticing, that at table their posteriors overflowed the straw-bottomed chairs and their breasts spilled out of their blouses? Or had I been so haunted by the story of the Great Famine that I did not see them becoming so overweight? Alice assured me that they were not all like that, that it was just one of my delusions, and that in the corner of the room, there was a table of athletic young men accompanied by wiry girls with bare navels.

Once our brief lunch ceremony in the inn was over, we went back out into the sea air and the amazing light on the bay and on Benbulben. The cemetery was close by, and was visible from the road. There was nothing theatrical about it, unlike Grand Bé in Saint-Malo where Chateaubriand is buried. Yeats wanted to enjoy his eternal repose at the base of his magic mountain in County Sligo. The church – I can say church, since in Ireland the word 'church' is used for both faiths – the church is unpretentious, built on the traditional model: a square steeple and a solid building. Inside it has the austerity of the reformed faith. People go there to sing or pray and not to be distracted by the surroundings. The emotion is tangible in the fresh air of the humble cemetery; there are few tombs and several are overrun by weeds or ivy. All over Ireland ivy has a terrifying voracity, choking trees, invading houses, covering tiles and even pushing open empty, dusty tombs with its all-consuming tentacles. Yeats lies there on the left-hand side, with no indication other than a black headstone and an epitaph known to all Irish people:

> *Cast a cold eye,*
> *On life, on death,*
> *Horseman, pass by!*

And his name with the dates that opened and closed his passage through this world: 13 June 1869 – 22 January 1939. The epigraph is taken from the last three lines of a poem written in France, at Cap-Martin, just over four months before his death.

> *Under bare Ben Bulben's head*
> *In Drumcliff churchyard Yeats is laid,*
> *An ancestor was rector there*
> *Long years ago; a church stands near,*
> *By the road an ancient Cross.*
> *No marble, no conventional phrase,*
> *On limestone quarried near the spot*
> *By his command these words are cut:*

> Cast a cold eye
> On life, on death.
> Horseman, pass by!

There are no flowers and no silly wreaths or photos, as there are for Catholics. No marble, just a plain black tombstone and an unmarked slab. Weeds wend their way around it, completing the triumph of eternal death, but Benbulben has been watching over the spot for thousands of years, a pharaonic mausoleum of dreams and marvels, a guardian of fairy work and witchcraft and Celtic legends that haunted the little boy, a boy who later became a man looking for his own soul and for the soul of a nation.

10.

BUILT IN THE fifteenth century by the MacCarthy clan, Blarney Castle is like all fortified castles: both boring and impressive. Its reputation extends far beyond the county of Cork. Under the walkway of its keep, one of the hand-cut stones juts out. It is said to have come from Scotland, from the same quarry as the famous Stone of Sconce, which was hidden under the coronation chair of the Kings of England for many years before being ceremoniously restored to its country of origin in 1996. The Blarney Stone gives the gift of eloquence to those who kiss it. The difficulty arises from the fact that it is accessible only through a trap in the walkway. Reaching it involves lying on your back and extending your head and neck into the void while hanging onto two handles encased in the wall.

With your back arched, your face comes level with the stone and, with the exception of hygiene fanatics (such people do exist), brushing your lips against it is enough to confer what is known as 'the gift of the gab' on you. The position is quite dangerous, especially if you suffer from vertigo. To avoid any possible falls, an attendant helps the pilgrims back on their feet. This attendant claims to give a hand to two thousand men and women each year.

Not all Irish people have visited Blarney. They rarely have need of its powers, and you are far more likely to meet foreigners there. Loquaciousness, or in biblical terms the power of the Word, is the ultimate weapon of people who refuse to submit to an oppressor. Those who possess the Word can dazzle or befuddle their masters. When liberty is restored, the Word remains a source of intoxication, a remedy against the burdens and vicissitudes of this world.

In the eighteenth century one traveller was already charmed by the art the Irish employ to scoff at reality. The Chevalier Bougrenet de la Tocnaye, a Breton gentleman who was exiled to London during the bloody years of the French Revolution, had tramped across Scotland and on his return published his observations, which were both witty and well judged. Heartened by the success of his first travelogue, he undertook a journey to Ireland in 1797.

La Tocnaye travelled light – a bundle containing his clothes and clean linen, a sword by his side and some letters of recommendation for like-minded gentlemen or bishops. His account of the trip, written in French, is all in good humour and perfectly honest. He lodged in castles, inns and sordid cottages, emerging from the latter covered with fleas and lice which he drowned by plunging naked into the icy waters of the Irish Sea or the Atlantic. Generously treated by some and given only a crust of rancid bread and dried herring by others, he delighted in listening to the natives. In Galway, the only port on the west coast, he discovered a city in the doldrums. A wine merchant was particularly eloquent: 'Before France knew how to make wine, we made it here in their stead.'

'How so?' La Tocnaye wondered. 'I have never seen any vines on my journey.'

'Oh sir, you are right! Vines have never been grown here, but in France the wine was simply grape juice, and we used to import it here to make it drinkable. Unfortunately the merchants of Bordeaux learned from us how to treat their grape juice and eventually worked out how to make wine as good as ours. They cut the ground from under our feet.'

La Tocnaye allowed the reader to imagine his response. Let us hope that he was sympathetic. Such matters allow no leeway for discussion. Two centuries later, Nicolas Bouvier recounted his visit to Clonmacnoise, which was a centre of spirituality and learning in the sixth century. It was a bitterly cold winter. The young caretaker of the site did not leave his log cabin, but he gave the only visitor of the day a booklet about the history of the abbey and, more precious still, a cup of burning hot tea.

'From the window', wrote Bouvier, 'I could see a couple of pheasants pecking on the road, which was striking because of all its useless turns. When I asked the caretaker why the road was traced in such an irregular fashion, he replied that in the past women laid down the stones on the paths and didn't like the wind to disturb their hair. When the wind turned, they turned also. This explanation was entirely satisfactory.'

The gift of the gab was given to the Irish not for any old reason, but so that they could bring irrefutable answers to an ignorant and irrational world. In their generosity, not only do they dream of an ethical ideal freed from overwhelming logic, they also invite those who speak to them to accompany them on that route.

It is no surprise then to learn that an Irishman, and what's more a Northerner from Derry, had the wonderful idea of setting up a Museum of the Verbal Arts. The definition of verbal arts is a wide-ranging one. For Sam Burnside, its founder, the term can be divided into four categories – speaking, listening, reading and writing. Broadminded man that he is, he includes both the spoken voice and the singing voice in those categories. Ireland's greatest treasures, he says quite rightly, are its stories, myths, legends and jokes: its humour and its writings. Everything comes back to that. Sam Burnside wants his Museum of Verbal Arts to ignite people's imagination, and he outlines its function thus: 'The imagination must be used without arbitrary limits. We must imagine and share our visions with others.' The wine merchant in Galway would certainly have liked the conclusion of the founder of the Museum of the Verbal Arts: 'When you're being spoken to, you must listen ... One of the characteristics of Ulster people is that they listen rarely and badly. Listen, I'll say it again, listen when you're spoken to.'

The visitors to the Museum of Verbal Arts will learn with pleasure and stupefaction that speaking is a means of communication that is easier and faster than reading, the post office and the media in general.

FOR SOME TIME NOW, Leslie R. has been supplying me with stories.

'We don't teach them anything,' he says, looking at the dogs playing in the yard. 'They know everything, but for some foolish reason that can be traced back to Paradise, they were expelled and they lost the power of speech. As is the case for men, the curse still holds. Sometimes you would think they have got round it. At about ten years old they don't bark anymore. They mumble and you'd have to be a complete idiot not to understand what they're saying. A dog who lived to thirty would be able to talk as clearly as you.'

'And as you!'

'Oh, it's none of our doing. Our ancestors were chased out of Paradise for a venial sin. An apple! I have whole baskets full of apples every year in my little orchard and no one from the village can be bothered to come and pick them up. When I was a child, my parents would ring the schoolmaster and he would send the children out of class with big bags to collect the apples. Now, I can tell them to help themselves as much as I like, but they prefer their apples nice and red and smooth, and sealed in cellophane from the supermarket. And so my apples – which are very good apples, I promise you – my poor apples rot on the ground and I am driven to despair by drunken wasps that come right up to the house. No, it's nothing to do with you or me. Our parents brought us up properly. You write books and I don't do anything for a living but let out my grass to neighbours, and, almost just for the fun of it, I look after dogs and spend my evenings reading books about animals and nature.'

He is a tall spare man with long legs, not a hint of fat in his face, and parchment-like skin that clings so tightly to his cheekbones, jaw and nose that you'd think it was ready to explode and reveal a mortuary mask underneath. He still has some teeth. His well-trimmed hair is perfectly white. When we meet each other in the forest, he's always wearing a cloche-shaped tweed hat, a pair of faded jeans and a woollen check shirt. Nothing else, even if it's raining – he must go home soaked to the skin.

'I'm like the dogs,' he says. 'The heat of my body dries me off and, like the dogs, I never get a cold or the flu.'

There is no point in trying to catch him out; he always knows what you're about.

On the lapel of his only jacket, worn when he goes to mass, you can make out a tarnished badge in Christ's image – the pioneer pin, a symbol of abstinence. He drinks nothing but tea. I have never been inside his house. We met in Pollnaknockaun Wood, where he walks his dogs and the dogs he looks after, and where I walk my dog too. The forest is said to be a 'wildlife reserve'. A sign at the entrance claims that you can see deer, pheasants, woodpeckers (I doubt that), long-eared owls (my book *The Guide to Birds in Europe* warns that it is difficult to see them, but from time to time you can hear their twit twoo), woodcocks and *one* couple of sparrow-hawks there. The deer are easy to see in winter. From a distance. Only one ever came close to me, a proud male with magnificent antlers. We stared at each other for two or three minutes.

'I know him,' said Leslie. 'He is called Icarus and you'll understand why when you see him jump a ditch. He flies. Naturally, I only meet him if I am by myself. He hates the dogs – his scent drives them mad. There are too many does and not enough males for him to fight. The race is in danger. Nobody really looks after them.'

When I have the pleasure of bumping into Leslie, we walk companionably along together. His cosmopolitan pack runs ahead of him while my sensible dog remains by my side. With his stick Leslie frees up a drain or whips aside a bramble bush when one of the branches is hanging across our path. If I stop to look through a gap in the trees at the steely mirror of Lough Derg and the mauve mountains of Slieve Aughty, he carries on, slowing his step. The gaps are the result of the inevitable felling programme of the company that manages Pollnaknockaun (not an easy name but I can't help that). In the wake of the tightly planted pine trees, nothing but a battlefield remains – horribly mutilated trunks, chopped branches, deep tracks furrowed by the machinery. Some birch trees, ashs and holm oaks have been spared. Without the protection of the pine trees they are terribly fragile. The slightest gust of wind leaves them trembling like reeds.

One day, while walking behind his two wirehaired pointers, his two labradors, a setter, a springer, two fox-terriers, two hounds and some harriers, Leslie said: 'These two at the back are mine. I saved them from the pack when they were puppies. Otherwise they would have died at the age of five or six. The hunting master is too demanding. But it's true that the harriers love it! It's better to live a short life intensely than a long life like a larva.'

Who was he thinking of?

'The dogs' instinct is down to themselves, whereas my parents taught me a lot. I even went to university in Galway. Oh, with no great enthusiasm. One day, instead of going to class, I was wandering down Shop Street when a dog made a sound just like a human and crossed the road at top speed, sat at my feet, blocked my way and held out his paw to me. It wasn't the spontaneous action that upset me, it was the look in his eyes. Dark, shiny and so intense, so human, that my heart stopped beating – it was the look my brother had, and he'd died two years previously from a terrible illness. This dog had the same tender warm look and he was begging me to take him with me. I said, 'Bill, is it you?' I'm not saying he replied but I swear that his eyes tried to talk. When dogs were hunted out of Paradise, they were also prevented from shedding even a single tear.'

'What a punishment,' I said. 'There's nothing like a good cry.'

'Bill,' he said. 'Yes, I named him after my brother. Bill stayed with me. Nobody came looking for him. I still wonder if he had a master. If you ask how I explain that, I have given up trying to explain anything since that day. And it suits me just fine. Bill died like my brother. Before he passed on, I told him that he wasn't to come back again, that it was too painful. We will see each other again, but not on this earth.'

LESLIE LIVES in his family home, a two-storey Georgian house. The walls are made of dressed stone, the roof is made of slates and it has sash windows. Everything is grey, very grey and darkly boring. You can tell that it was a gentleman's home just one or two generations ago. The kennels are in the old stables. They are the only part of the house that seems to be modern and comfortable. The rest? I know nothing about it and haven't been invited in, not even for the traditional nice cup of tea. If I hoot the horn at the gate, I see him moving from room to room, pulling the curtains, even the shutters and closing everything behind him, turning the key twice in the lock, locking the front door and taking the lock off the kennel, opening the door of the van for the labradors, pointers, setters and harriers to rush furiously inside, barking joyfully.

'THE PRESENCE of Bill disturbed me so much that I stopped going to class. During the five years that his reincarnation lasted, I struggled to break down the barriers. The only thing I asked him to do was to say a word, just one word, maybe just a 'yes' or a 'no', but preferably a two-syllable word, my name.

It was on the tip of his tongue. I never gave up. As he was dying, at the most touching moment when his eyes were begging me – you know that instant when a suffering animal asks why, why? – I thought that the absurd, cruel decree of Creation would waver. Well it didn't. Like my brother Bill before him, my dog Bill died of a terrible disease.'

A FEW MINUTES away from Abbey and Pollnaknockaun, Derrycrag Wood extends over almost a thousand hectares on the flank of a hill. Initially it was an oak forest, but it was destroyed in the eighteenth century for the needs of the Royal Navy. It has been replanted with evergreen trees. In this peaty soil the pines have grown to fairytale heights. The fauna is unobtrusive – some young deer, and a very civilized fox who stands in the middle of the path and stares at intruders. The trouble with Derrycrag is the deceptiveness of its paths. Although you may find your way back easily enough on your first visit, the second time round everything becomes confused: the paths run into dead clearings; huge ferns and laurel bushes cover the tracks. An intruder finds himself trapped by a smothering and dizzying vegetation that closes up behind him. The next time you return with markers to flag out your route – red ribbons that you tie onto the low branches at the crossings – and you think you are in control. A week later you are lucky if you come across two or three of the ribbons. To do that, you have to climb back up the hill through the woods. It's possible, but irritating, and your only consolation is that when you draw near the exit, you find yourself face to face with a small stocky man wearing a cap with earflaps. He is loading sheets of moss onto a cart pulled by a donkey and stops to stick a pinch of snuff up his nostrils, sniffs and replies: 'What am I doing with the moss? It's for the graves, of course. That's nice fresh moss now. Poor Tony Murphy will love it. He did tell me before he died that he'd like a good layer of it!'

Good manners always force you to be grief-stricken at the death of a human being, even if you know nothing about them and wish to know nothing about them unless they reappear to tell you what life is like on the other side.

'Ah, he's dead, is he?'

'He was forty-five years old! After a whole life spent without a drink, a smoke or a woman. When I think of the good time he could have had, I feel sorry for him. If he had smoked, drunk and fucked he might still be with us today. The funeral is this afternoon at 4 o'clock. Are you coming?'

With a certain degree of mental reservation, some promises are not very binding.

'I KNOW HIM,' Leslie said the following day. 'I think he's called Seamus. He earns his living with the dead. When no one dies in X, he lives off credit in pubs and shops. He's one of those people you should never ask questions. His answers are too long. He might have told you that people get lost easily in Derrycrag, and why.'

The reason for this is perfectly clear. In the nineteenth century a banshee was living at the edge of the wood. When she died, the priest refused to allow her to be buried in the churchyard. Well-intentioned people interred her somewhere in the clearing. Nobody knows where. When an innocent person dares to stray into the forest she draws them into her web, and, if they have one or two dogs, she puts a spell on them. The banshee can have no effect on the walker if they stop at the Virgin's stream. A path leads down between the trees to the water just before it swells up and turns into a waterfall that thunders into the lake. Right down at the bottom, on the edge, at the side of a pond in which a trickle of water flows that cures illnesses of the eyes, stands a plaque with a glass-fronted tabernacle on top. Behind the glass a Virgin figure dressed in blue and white holds dried flowers in her arms. All around her are scraps of paper with requests or death notices. To ensure that she protects the walker against the witch's tricks, it is wise to place a few coins in a tin begging-bowl. However, more than ten cents is a sign of vulgarity. The protection of the Virgin Mary is not to be sold to the highest bidder. It seems that you are safer still if you hang some pieces of cloth or a strip of your own linen to one of the low-lying branches of the holm oak. The latter will protect you against the curses of the the old woman.

WE ARRANGED to meet at Derrycrag. 'Without the dogs,' he clarified, 'if we want to meet *the* fox. You haven't had lots of time to look at him. He is going grey now. He's a loner and they say he is the soul of the banshee. If you let them go, the dogs run after him and he leads them into the depths of the forest. And they are never seen again. Be it true or false, it's better not to take any risks. I think it's true that the fox is possessed by the spirit of the banshee. During her time on earth, she suffered at lot at the hands of men. Doors were closed on her face, she was starved, and even the poor cabin that she lived in was burnt to the ground. The terrible things about those cursed women is that nobody goes to help them in peace to stop them dying of hunger. Children are trained to hate and fear them, to throw stones at them or to lay rubbish at their doors. It's no wonder they defend themselves by casting spells on people! With the foxes it's the same thing. They attack sheep because no one leaves them any bones to chew on. They make the fields, the forests and their setts stink so as to escape the hounds. They are killed for no reason – just for the pleasure of killing even though they are inedible.

My family came over from England in the seventeenth century, and we have always got on well with foxes even though for generations each man of the family had his own pack and was master of the hunt. But they didn't hunt foxes, just hares and deer. I don't know when the tradition started, and it probably happened little by little, but whenever one of my ancestors died, that very morning a bevy of foxes would appear at the gate. They would yelp in memory of the dead person for a few minutes, then they'd head off in a straight line quietly, one after the other. Somewhere around 1900, my grandfather disappeared. Just like that! He left on horseback without his things and didn't leave a note. That very evening the horse returned to the stable still saddled, stirrups low and bridle around his neck. Everyone thought that my grandfather had had an accident; the ponds and lakes were dragged and the surrounding woods searched. Nothing. It was as if he had vanished into thin air. For the first time in generations the foxes did not come yowling at the gate. After about five or six years my grandmother decided to remarry. She was young and pretty and had only two children. The parish priest – we're Catholics, there aren't many of us round here – refused to celebrate the marriage until the foxes came yowling at the gate. A few years later, at dawn, my grandmother was woken by the foxes, and that very morning the postman came with a letter saying my grandfather had just died in Jakarta. The priest celebrated the marriage within the week. You won't believe any of that but I do and I think other people in the area do too. As long as someone believes in something, that thing exists.'

WE WALKED for more than an hour without meeting the greying fox. At one point Leslie realized that he had taken the wrong turning down one of the forest paths and he laughed.

'The banshee has got us. I can hear her cackling. And we forgot to ask the Virgin Mother for her protection! The sky has got so dark that the last couple of minutes, it's going to try to drown us, and that will be our punishment. I hope you're not too disappointed. In any case, you really should get a lungful of fresh air every day.'

22.

WE HAD ARRANGED to meet at 1pm. I arrived a minute early and saw that he was right behind me on the road. It was so unlike the Irish that I was astounded. The weather was unusual too; it was divine, and brighter than anywhere else in the world. The tide was advancing up the ria, and two or three hours later the flock of swans who had taken refuge at the head would descend majestically to the mouth where the freshwater met the sea. Seagulls were dandling in the mud. On the quay, Moran's had set up tables with parasols, but we chose to eat inside in an alcove, as we could see the ria and the terrace just as well from there. Unfortunately, no one there was worthy of our attention.

Although it took him over an hour to get there from his home in County Leitrim, John McGahern knew Moran's well, and he'd loved the idea of meeting there for a few oysters (they weren't quite in season yet, by December they would be delectable). The young girl who served us was not the tall willowy one with plump cheeks who wore very short mini-skirts over her admirable legs. The author of *The Pornographer* would not get distracted during our discussion. That novel, published twenty-five years earlier, left him with a sulphurous reputation that was much envied by his Irish colleagues. He ended up losing his teaching job and had to go and live in London to wait for the storm to blow over.

The Pornographer is not a pornographic novel, though; it is a novel *about* pornography and the descent into hell of a professional writer of books to be read with one hand. In John McGahern's novels and short stories, women initially play a strangely passive role before their submission is plucked away to reveal a pitiless harshness, while the conquering male finds himself alone, abandoned and miserable on the platform, waiting for a train that will never come.

As we sat in our lodge with a bottle of muscadet waiting for our oysters to arrive, I got a better look at John. To be honest, when I first saw him at a conference at the 'Etonnants Voyageurs Festival' in Saint-Malo, I found him quite ordinary until he was annoyed by a perfectly stupid remark made by a member of the audience, who reprimanded him for ignoring the problem posed by the troubles in Northern Ireland between republicans and loyalists, and a burst of anger trans-formed his face in a way no one expected from such a quiet man. He pointed out, and quite rightly too, that a writer is above all free to make his own choices, and that what he thought about the bloody stages of this endless civil war was nobody's business, especially not a cretin who knew nothing about it at all.

That was enough for me to take a greater interest in him, and now he was sitting in front of me, busy buttering a slice of brown bread, and tasting his first oyster. His face was oval, with falsely candid blue eyes that twinkled with intelligence. As soon as the conversation turned humorous, his expression gave him away and he became smirking, ribald, or after a two second blankness, worried that he should stray too far from the truth – every Irishman's forbidden fruit.

His most recent book, *That They May Face the Rising Sun*, had perhaps a shade misleadingly been called a 'novel'. I have a little difficulty in accepting the idea that it is a work of fiction since my dominant impression is that his characters resemble any one of my neighbours in County Galway. I would prefer to have called the work 'novels', because it develops like a fresco, finely interweaving members of a community who live by the side of a lake. Nothing so profoundly human and so unvarnishedly honest has ever been written about rural Irish society. It rises above the blackness with which Irish literature usually speaks about its world, about its love-hate relationship with the Catholic Church and about the suffering it cultivates irremediably with such masochism.

'The priests who played such a role in Irish life are fading farther and farther into the past,' he said. 'Still, we shouldn't forget their courage and tenacity in educating a nation that had been relatively crude until the Celtic Revival at the end of the nineteenth century.'

We spoke briefly about the paedophile priests issue. The fact that there were so many of them was just as surprising as the fact that the bishop of Galway was caught embezzling money from a charity for the upkeep of his American mistress and illegitimate son. This was going far beyond the perversions Irish writers were accused of and censored for both openly and, what's worse, in secret. Molly Bloom's monologue in Joyce's *Ulysses* has never had as pernicious an effect on its readers' lives as the forced intimacies of the clergy has had on the youth of the country. Irish literature can always justify itself as having brought the country back to 'its' infinitely fallible truth.

In *That They May Face the Rising Sun* the most poignant character in the community is the man we see least. He has been marked by a fatal sign – that of unrequited love, exile, and death by a heart attack. In the book there is no lamentation of his death, no nervous breakdowns, perhaps not even any tears, but he is treated like a mummy: make-up, grooming, Sunday best. His family and former friends gather round his body and drink to his eternal rest. Without quite rejoicing, believers and non-believers alike share the same conviction: our stay on this earth is just an unfortunate phase before our true birth, when we will finally be reunited with our loved ones and delivered, like them, from all human miseries great and small, the small ones often being the worst of all. People drink at the wake. After the cemetery they meet again in a pub, not necessarily to speak about the dead person. People don't say 'Johnny is dead': they say 'he passed on', come from no one knows where and gone on to limbo and universal reconciliation, which he will surely reach if he is buried to face the rising sun. In a recent enquiry, 86 per cent of young Irish people said they believed in God, perhaps mixing up belief in the resurrection and belief in an all-indulgent God. Priests, who have played such a great role in the Irish novel, scarcely appear at all in McGahern's work – they are asked to perform baptisms, weddings and funerals. In *That They May Face the Rising Sun*, paradoxically, the priest's benevolent and consoling role is occupied by Ruttledge, a newcomer to the community, and we learn that he is perhaps a defrocked priest or, at least, a seminarian who left before being ordained. *That They May Face the Rising Sun* is a milestone in the slow rise of the Irish novel after the thunderclap of Joyce's *Ulysses*. McGahern has erased the reality that was steering the novel away from its real objectives. He has also erased time, which makes such a heavy impact on the characters in his world. Yesterday and tomorrow no longer exist, and if it wasn't for the admirable characters the novelist depicts, each day would just be an increasingly pale copy of the preceding one.

We finished our oysters. John ordered two-dozen more to take away with him. He'd barely had one glass of muscadet, and he refused the coffee because it makes him nervy. He fixed his tweed cap on his head with the peak up at a slight angle; his pale blue eyes had a crafty look about them, like a writer drawing in his readers. We took our leave of each other on the quay; the tide was already high. On the opposite bank a dozen cows were lying in the grass.

'I have a few cows,' he said.

Ireland is a land where the city dweller likes to play at being a farmer, and maybe vice versa. At the end of *That They May Face the Rising Sun* Bill Evans, who has always lived a hand-to-mouth existence earning his living from odd jobs, and whom we have seen ten times carrying pails of lakewater, or begging cigarettes and a half of beer, leaves his humble role – he goes off to live in the town and wears a waistcoat and tie for his round of goodbyes. The sight is so stupefying that no one in the community mentions it to him.

WE WENT our separate ways. McGahern headed for County Leitrim and I went off to south Galway, both of us regretful, I think, not to have broken the surface of what we were talking about.

'You must come to Foxfield.'

Yes, certainly. I'd love to see his books – 'show me what you read and I'll tell you who you are' – and the lake he'd set up house by thirty years before. It will be for another time after this friendly introduction.

IN FACT, I had to wait six months and I scarcely found out anything else about that deeply reserved man. It was true that the shelves in his house in Foxfield were weighed down with books, but the names and the titles were difficult to make out. The room where he worked was a monk's cell of two by four metres. The desk was a simple table made of light-wood, facing the wall. McGahern doesn't allow the landscape to disturb him.

On Sunday 2nd January 2005, we were in Foxfield. The most disturbing thing of all was that Foxfield didn't exist. Before leaving, I looked for it on the most recent Michelin map of Ireland, and it was nowhere to be seen. On a map dating from thirty years earlier you can find Foxfield between Fernagh and Keshcarrigan: just eight tiny letters, without even a spot to indicate a hamlet. On all the other maps Foxfield has disappeared. What must it feel like to live in a place that no longer exists, which has only existed perhaps in the imagination of a cartographer or in a story of fairies and witches? Nothing on the road indicates that a cataclysm has taken place, or a quake that might have swallowed up a whole community. On the contrary, County Leitrim is a model of bucolic peace. To the north stand the Iron Mountains, visible in the crystalline light of winter, flecked with snow on the peaks and flanks. Between Mohill and Fernagh the road winds tenderly around lakes and ponds lined with beech trees and silver birches. Timid houses huddle among bay trees, ivy and climbing vines; flower-baskets hang from the windows of the pubs and over the doors. Relying on the old map, I headed west at Fernagh in the direction of Carrick-on-Shannon (or Cora Droma Druisc, if you prefer). To no avail. A young blonde girl on a bike pointed out a rundown pub to me, next to a commanding church with white clapboard walls that looked far more Scandinavian than Irish. I called McGahern and he came to meet me. Ten minutes later we were reunited and I followed him, first down a track that was easy to follow, then down another one that was wild and rutted, following the line of the green-bronze lake where little waves were lapping the shore. The white house, an old farmhouse built on one level, was at the top of a slope. The narrow windows of the façade looked out onto the lake, whose basin looked like it could well have been the old crater of a volcano.

'It's very deep,' McGahern replied. 'Very deep. It's filled from an underground source. I used to fish there when we moved here in the beginning, but not any more.'

He didn't hunt either, although wild birds abounded in that part of Leitrim, unlike south Galway where the bogs had been drained, the hedges levelled and the wildlife massacred, with the help of European Union funds. In Leitrim there were woodcock, snipe, mallards, pheasants, lapwings, and migrating snow geese land on the edges of the lake.

'And crows,' said Madeline McGahern, who was slim with a beautiful, intelligent face and short, grey hair.

If they are not often mentioned, it is because in the Irish sky the spiralling flights of myriads of croaking crows herald the devilment of the night.

OVER DINNER, John told the story of an irresistible congress that had taken place five or six years earlier in Portumna, very close to where I live, and that I knew nothing about. Almost a thousand people got together to save the countryside from increasing urbanization and the cynicism of property developers: ecologists, politicians, local representatives looking for support, defenders of the nomads who destroy official and unofficial campsites, friends of the forest or of foxes.

'In the end,' he said, 'if the speakers were to be believed, Ireland would be no more than a giant road network, a pile of houses each more hideous than the next. They were destroying what they had come to defend, each one of them – their demands were rarely very pure, perfectly anarchic in their aims, and just as damaging for the countryside as for everyday life. The congress ended with them rubbing their hands together, having defended the interests of their electors, their representatives or their corruptors. As is usually the case in congresses of that sort, nothing arose from this assault on demagogy. The following day, the *Irish Independent* published my murderous article on the congress on the front page. And all their ruinous, catastrophic projects have been forgotten about, thank God. Since then no one invites me to anything anymore.'

We talked about his collection of short stories. I couldn't remember a single one of them that wasn't full of despair. 'My Love, My Umbrella' was adapted as an opera.

'It was a disaster … Really terrible. The idea of setting to music the encounter of a man and a woman fornicating despondently behind a carriage door under an umbrella would never have crossed my mind. Perhaps I was wrong to allow it go ahead.'

McGahern's short stories, even more than his novels, reveal a lot about the mixture of pity and cruelty with which he dissects the human heart. Love is not in question; it is life that is sordid. The inhibitions, the silence, the moral squalor of the lonely speak of a society which in *That They May Face the Rising Sun* has got rid of its fears and some of its certainties. Contrary to many novelists of his generation (he is seventy years old), McGahern has observed the change in Irish society over the past thirty years. It's a completely different world to the one he portrayed in his first novels. The windows are open; a strong wind has blown away the consequences of a past that obsessed people for too long. The anger of the 'terrible beauty' roused by Yeats and the authors of the Irish Revival has been laid to rest. Since we mentioned Yeats, McGahern gave a cutting opinion:

'Yes, a poet, probably even a great poet, but his prose is illegible, emphatic and awkward.'

'And his plays?'

'Tedious.'

On my way out, I noticed that we had studiously avoided the ritual topics of Joyce and Beckett. And the French writers? Flaubert and Maupassant met with his approval. Out of the Americans, he liked Hemingway and Faulkner's short stories.

'I've just finished a book,' he said, as we were about to say goodbye.

'A novel?'

'No. Different things, memories. Nothing about writers. No. About my father and my mother. My father was a guard and he lived in a barracks thirty miles from my mother, who taught in the local primary school. They managed to have five children all the same.'

Does there come a time in a writer's life when, after masking and transforming all that he holds most dear and that inspires his work, the desire to write about it openly at last becomes irresistible?

12.

SAINT BRENDAN, son of Finloch, nephew of Alti of the Eoghen family and pupil of Saint Ita of Kileedy, was born in Munster at an unknown date, probably towards the end of the sixth century.

On board a curragh, a big boat made out of seal and shark skin and waterproofed with pitch and fish glue, Brendan was the first explorer of the Atlantic world. With a crew of seven vigorous monks, he sailed the ocean and the seas for seven years, bringing spiritual succour to edenic isles populated by hermit people – *The Land of the Promise of Saints, The Paradise of Birds*. To the primitive world, he revealed the word of Christ and the vision of eternal bliss.

His narrative, *Navigatio Brendani*, is the story of his expeditions beyond the horizon. At times with oars, at other times pushed by the wind blowing the square sail, the curragh of Saint Brendan opened the Atlantic world to Christianity. Legend has it that before Christopher Columbus left for Cipango, he came to Ireland to listen to the reminiscences of a sailor who claimed to have, like Saint Brendan, landed on the shore of an unknown land beyond the horizon. A quotation he borrowed from Dante's Purgatory chapter of the *Divine Comedy* is even more explicit:

'He came to shore with his clean-lined skiff, so light that it barely skimmed the water ... At its tiller, the famous ferryman stood upright. Everything about him emanated happiness; and inside more than a hundred spirits sat ...' *Navigatio Brendani* is one of those books that will go on forever. Poetic, learned, inspired, it lends the imagination to terrestrial and heavenly wonders. Each reader can make it their own.

THE SKY is torn between blue and gold. The west winds fall silent. At Moher, the ocean is gently licking the cliffs, and on the strand in Lahinch, the rollers die with spray on their lips. Saint Brendan has hoisted his sail and is standing in the stern with arms crossed. His red beard is blazing in the light. Beyond this point the world of men no longer exists; it is the kingdom of God, defended by sea monsters. To ward off these monsters without killing them – oh, no, they mustn't be killed, even if they are sent by the Evil One – Saint Brendan has been sharpening an invincible arm since his childhood, white hot, thin as a needle, strong as iron, shining like a bolt of lightning:

his faith. When he brandishes it, the tempest will be quelled and monsters will flee, or perhaps they will escort the travellers right to the threshold of the great gate where God waits, with a touch of impatience, for the son of Erin. The proud monk will tell Him what is happening on earth – men are cold, they bleed and suffer; no one on the horizon is listening to their prayers. Saint Brendan hasn't left to say pleasant things to God. He is going to tell Him about the Vikings who are ravaging the coasts, about the rain that is drowning the harvests, about the suffocating fog, about the temptations that harass humans and provoke them to sin, about the women and children who are shivering on the red moors. Yes, what are You doing, Lord, for those who adore You and obey Your commandments? At what games do You waste Your time, instead of looking after us? A warm wind has risen and fills out the square sail. The boat of tar and cloth groans in the swell. Saint Brendan neither eats nor drinks. He wants to present himself to God in a wasted state, like a dying man with glassy eyes, like those who are begging in vain for help.

Through days and nights, Saint Brendan, whose beard is now grey with sea salt, knows that he is going the right way. The Ocean is as infinite as the power of the potentate of the hereafter. The horizon is in constant retreat, tinted at sunset with a fire that is put out by the foam at night and reborn from the ashes in the morning, onto the crew's backs. This troubles the men. They ought to be able to smell burning, feel a shower of soot raining down on them; but the only smell is that of the ocean, and the air is as pure and fresh as it was in the beginning of the world. God is an enchanter, thinks Saint Brendan, but we are stronger; we believe in Him more than He believes in Himself. If He has become a prisoner of His own spells, we shall deliver Him, we shall restore His power and He will help mankind again, instead of strumming that lute of His.

When the continent is in sight, Saint Brendan opens his arms wide. Standing thus at the stern of his boat, he looks like a cross covered with sea crystals. His eyes are flashing, aflame. God is not far. God is on the coast and has lit a fire, and breeze is twisting its smoke into spirals. A mournful lament rises from the crew, who have abandoned their oars. The boat enters a clear bay, and runs aground on the sand. Brendan holds out his arms, palms open, offering the misery of the world to the Almighty for him to remedy it. The Almighty emerges from the cloud of smoke. He is a thin red man with feathers in his hair, paint on his cheeks. He is carrying a bow, stops to stretch it and fires an arrow that lands flaccidly on the deck, just missing the saint in his ecstasy.

'This is not God!' the monk exclaims. 'We have gone off course. Let us return to Erin, where all is pleasant, pale and green. God could never live on these ungrateful lands. God is within us, in the garden of our souls … Turn around … Quickly … This may be Hell.'